Michael "Robt

email: robbo1201

Behind The Band

About the author

Michael Robinson had a difficult childhood and was diagnosed with schizoaffective disorder at the age of seventeen.

At the age of twenty, Robinson joined the Fourth Battalion Parachute regiment, and later the Third Battalion Prince Of Wales's own regiment. Upon passing out, he was awarded 'most improved recruit.'

Later into his military career, Robinson volunteered for the arduous 'Cambrian patrol", a type of special forces training, with a view towards joining the S.A.S. However during deployment in the Brecon Beacons, Robinson succumbed to hypothermia, and was ultimately sacked from the army on Christmas Eve after they had looked into his medical records.

From here, Robinson ended up in Hull prison and later was locked up indefinitely under section 37/41. He remained locked up for about three years and on release wrote about his experiences in his autobiography 'Sectioned: The Book The NHS Tried To Ban' on Amazon Kindle.

As well as a soldier, other jobs Robinson has done include drummer for two successful groups, carer at a special needs school, chef, bouncer, driver and minder for a Hull escort agency. Also he has an

NVQ in catering, a diploma in Uniform Public Services, and has read law with criminology at university.

Robinson has been married to his long term partner, Julie, for eleven years. He continues to support mental health campaigns with help from his local MP and other government agencies. This includes working with the Heads Together campaign, Mind, and other mental health charities.

(YouTube: "heads together campaign michael 'robbo' robinson")

He regularly helps out the homeless in Hull and other persons/groups in need where he can.

Other books by Robinson include:

- Sectioned- The book the NHS tried to ban. (Autobiography)
- The Killing Moon (Fiction)
- Dirty Laundry- Confessions of an escort agency minder (Autobiography)
- Thief Taker (Fiction)
- Eliminator- Part of the Rob Foster series (Fiction)

All of the above are available on Amazon.

Forward

When setting out on this new project, there is a few people I need to thank, without whom Behind The Band would not be possible.

I should point out, I am dyslexic therefore without my typist, whom types, reads back, administrates, then this book would not be written. Forever in debt to your dedication, flexibility and trust in this project.

I'd like to thank all the groups I have been involved with, it's funny but you become a musical family.

I'd also like to thank my family, in particularly, my wife Julie, for not only putting up with me, the late nights, the hectic lifestyle and also my snoring. Without you, I'd be lost Babe.

Lastly, I'd like to acknowledge my Grandmother, who I lost a few years ago. You're always with me in spirit.

Behind The Band

Chapter One- In the beginning

Rock and roll, it's a magical beast. When does anyone first fall in love with rock and roll? It becomes your mistress, your little sister, your wife, your big brother. It's there for you in your dark days, it's there for you on the hot summer days, we play music at weddings and funerals, we listen to it as were going to work, we listen to it on a night out or even getting ready. I know one thing, the first time you hear it, it changes your life, in some cases it changes the direction of your life. Once when you thought you wanted to be a footballer or a police man or even an astronaut, when you hear rock and roll, everything changes. It's like a calling in the same way a vicar becomes called to a church or a nurse decides she wants to be a midwife. It's also a way of life. You don't have to listen to some big fat baldy old fart to take this box and stick it in a corner, on a mind numbing leave your brain at the door factory job.

Rock and roll has this outlaw-ish image to it. You can do what you want to do. It's all about sticking it to the man. That day you're told you get a pay cut, in rock and roll you can say shove your job. Once it's in your blood, it never leaves.

The first time I discovered rock and roll, I was about eleven. I was in the first year of secondary school and a girl called Vicky, whose last name I cannot remember, lent me a cassette. The cassette was Def Leppard's "Hysteria" and it was a Saturday afternoon and I played it back to back on my Mum's kitchen radio tape player whilst she was out shopping.

The other thing I remember, is seeing this group with long hair, stone washed denim jeans with shreds in, ripped t-shirts with the sleeves missing. A lot of people say when they first hear rock and roll, they sing in the mirror with a tennis racket, with me it was an old pool cue case which was my guitar as I danced around the living room. That's the first time I clearly remember hearing rock.

I'd always known about rock from a very young age. My old man was a rocker and would often come home pissed up on a Saturday afternoon and play his Deep Purple records louder than thunder. In later years, Mum would use it as one of her grounds for divorce as she told the judge Dad's music frightened the children. To be fair, any three year old that had to sit through "Child in time" by Deep Purple, with the insane screaming, of singer Ian Gillan, it's little wonder that it frightened me and my older sister. Other groups I knew about at this age through Dad included Thin Lizzy, Fleetwood Mac, ZZ Top, Led Zeppelin and of course everyone knew who The Beatles were.

Later down the line, after the divorce, I would go away with Dad in his truck and he introduced me to Van Halen's 1984 album, this included hits like "Jump", "Panama" and "Hot for teacher", which leads me to wanting to play guitar.

Dad and I were away somewhere in Scotland, when I asked him to play "1984". The cassette had been played endlessly on the journey, however at Christmas, the previous year, my sister had bought Dad the cassette of Van Halen's first album, simply called "Van Halen".

Instead of putting on "1984", Dad said "Have a listen to this Son." I learnt what playing a guitar really meant when I heard Eddie Van Halen's solo called "Eruption". Even 35 years after I first heard "Eruption", I knew I wanted to play guitar. To this day, I rate Eddie Van Halen, the greatest guitarist that ever lived. Not that other guitarists weren't good or outstanding even, but what Eddie did and at that time, I suspect, meant a lot of would be guitarists decided it was time to take up plumbing. Eddie was that good, he did things nobody else did and he invented a whole genre of playing known as 'Tapping'.

Being the new Eddie Van Halen, all I needed was a guitar. I would have been around twelve at the time and the rock magazine that was popular at the time was called " Raw". Inside there was an advertisement for an electric guitar and a practice amp and looking back I think it was roughly one hundred quid. It would have been ideal, however I was with my uncle when I showed the advertisement to my Mum. Mum looked at my uncle and said " Are they safe?" at which point my Uncle Julian replied " Not if it's not earthed". At that point my wish was shattered and I knew I was not going to be the new Eddie Van Halen that year.

However the bug for rock and roll had not waned. If anything the desire in me grew stronger. At the school disco on a Tuesday evening you had two hours of New Kids On The Block, Kylie Minogue and other Stock Aitken and Waterman shit, however the last half hour was set aside for the real music. Enter AC/DC. The first time I heard the live version of "Whole Lotta Rosie" was at the school disco and even the two DJs would get out of the booth, start a mosh and bang our heads together. All the time, the posh kids, the jocks and the snotty girls would stand around us wondering what the hell we was doing. It was like we was worshipping some heavy metal cult. They just did not get it, not that it mattered.

At that point I would go to various outlets, with whatever pocket money I had. Buy up all the AC/DC records. AC/DC itself was like a magical beast, Angus the guitarist dressed as a school boy was something you would hope would shock your parents. To this day AC/DC are my favourite group. I've had the pleasure of seeing them live three times, twice at Donnington. Other groups I found around this time were Aerosmith, Bon Jovi, Alice Cooper, Poison and Mötley Crue. Also, I had found out about the Donnington 'Monsters of rock' festival at Donnington Park. This leads me to another story.

Chapter Two- Early gigs

I would have been about thirteen and it was 1990. The line up for the Donnington 'Monsters of Rock' festival this year included Thunder as the openers, The Quireboys, Poison, Aerosmith, (Who were riding high on their comeback album "Pump") and the headliners were Whitesnake. I was adamant, I was going, just as Mum was adamant I was not. Mum and Dad were divorced at this point and I was pretty much in the position where I could get away with a lot. Don't ask me how but I managed to save thirty five pounds for my ticket, thirty pounds for the ticket and five pounds for the coach. Back then in Hull, the music shop "Gough and Davy's", known in Hull as Goth's, not only sold instruments, they also sold tickets, which included coaches. Unbeknown to Mum, defiantly I handed over my thirty five pounds and was promptly rewarded with two tickets and a folder to keep them in. The ticket was then strategically placed under my pillow for the next three months.

The date for the gig was arriving and of course my big Sister knew everything about it and somehow persuaded me to tell Mum about my ticket and of course the answer was "You're not going and you'll have to sell the ticket." I should mention as well the whole concert was being played live on Radio One.

It was a battle of wills, although I did try to sell the ticket, there were no takers. I asked my Dad if he wanted it, but he wasn't interested. We also asked Moss, who is my Dad's best mate and a big

Whitesnake fan but again the answer was no. I had one more endeavour to try.

Viking Radio was the local radio station and was fairly new in Hull in the late eighties- early nineties. I rang and spoke to the two DJs on the phone in. I can't remember what they said, there was one guy and one lady and I explained my Mum would not let me go to the concert, both chuckled. However, they were good enough to put it on air that I had a ticket for sale. But again there were no takers. I am now a week before the concert and despite my endeavours one thing I was sure about, this ticket was not going to be wasted.

Many of my peers would say "Fuck your Mum, just go" even Moss' daughter said the same. I knew full well if I did just that, there would be a shit storm. After a lot of thought, I came to the conclusion 'Fuck it, let Mum kick off I'm going' and the Friday night before the concert Mum and her friend Ann went out for a drink together. As soon as they left the house I got into bed, I was determined, I was going.

Within an hour the phone rang, it was Ann, Mum's friend, basically after a bit of discussion in the pub Ann persuaded Mum that I should be allowed to go to the concert. Ann rang me to say if you get into bed, your Mum will let you go. I just answered "I'm already in bed." And she chuckled.

The day the concert arrived. Mum woke me up, it must've been about half past five in the morning, she offered to drive me to town to Ferensway, when in 1990 that was where you got the coaches to go to the concerts. (Now it's a monstrosity called Paragon Interchange and St Stevens.)

I felt very grown up getting on the bus all on my own with all these rockers, I'd of only been fourteen. Fortunately, I had made sandwiches the night before, however these only lasted about five minutes after the coach left Hull. In my pocket, I had about thirty pounds to buy a t-shirt and the obligatory twenty silk cut, the cigs that were popular at the time.

Eventually, we reached Donnington park race track and I'd never seen so many people in my life. Every one of them were rockers, it was like a calling to the mountain. I also remember it was a red hot day in August.

Donnington in them days, the crowd used to light fires, again health and safety put paid to that many years ago, but back then it was a ritual. I had never seen so many plastic containers flying through the air at the same time near the stage. If you was anywhere near the front you needed to have eyes in the back of your head. Half the time you never knew what was in these containers, however it was mainly wet, warm and yellow.

Tommy Vance was the DJ that hosted the event. In 1990 Tommy Vance had his own Radio one rock show on a Friday night and was a well know figure in the rock community. Also, back then people listened to Radio one.

All in all, it was a great day. Every band that came on to entertain the crowd were brilliant and of course I was in awe of all these famous faces that I had only ever seen on telly. Especially when it came to the later groups like Poison and Aerosmith (Aerosmith on this occasion were absolutely brilliant and even invited to the stage the Led Zeppelin guitarist, Jimmy Page).

As the sun started to fade, it was time for the headlines, Whitesnake. Just before the sun light faded they came to the stage. Singer David Coverdale walked on stage with his hand in the air saluting the audience as the rest of the group claimed their positions. It was like watching Gods from a different planet gracing us with their presence. I was pretty tired and pretty hungry at this point but I just watched in awe at every song and every solo. After two hours Whitesnake finished the set, with the track "Still of the night" then the obligatory fireworks.

Potentially, there could have been a drama on the way home, I managed to plough my way through the field where the coach was waiting. I knew it was the right coach because in the window it said

"Gough and Davy, Hull". However I was just about to board the bus when the doors shut and it was about to leave, I banged on the coach door, stepped on board and showed the hostess my ticket. Given my age, she was quite gentle with me, however what I did not realise more people had got on the coach back to Hull then had left in the morning. The hostess looked at my ticket, then turned to the driver and said " It's valid, you know" then she addressed the coach down the microphone and said "Whoever has not got a ticket must get off now." The coach remained silent and nobody took up the offer to alight. That was the first drama. The second drama was, I'd fallen asleep shattered on the way home and did not wake up until I was at Boothferry Road, Hull. I was supposed to get off in Brough, but again all's well that ends well. Alighting off the bus near the Costello's stadium, I found the nearest phone box I could (remember them?) and reversed the charges to my Mum to come and pick me up at half past four in the morning.

That was my first experience of a festival and for the next three years, I went religiously to the 'Monsters of Rock Festival', watching bands such as AC/DC, Iron maiden, Metallica, Mötely Crew, Wasp, the list goes on.

Also about this time, I started going to night clubs in Hull on the rock nights. Even though I was still at school and only about fourteen, I had long hair and I was tall for my age. One thing I was adamant about, I was going to be the next guitar God, the new Eddie Van Halen, I was going to be a rock star and I was going to form a band.

Not many of the kids at my school were rockers, in fact hardly any of them were. The truth was there was only two lads with long rock and roll hair in the whole year, I was one of them, the other was Chris Bodie. Soon, we became friends and we had lots of talks on the band we was going to form together, however that's all it ever was, talk. Nothing ever materialised between me and Bodie however, we both befriended each other but in later years this would end in disaster and tears.

Whist at school, I began song writing. Nothing in league with Noah Gallager or Kurt Cobain, however I was using my imagination and I was being creative. Unfortunately, at my school South Hunsley at that time to say you wanted a career in music was not only frowned upon by the establishment, as if it was a dirty word, you also were never encouraged to do anything musical or creative. The fact was at South Hunsley unless you came from an affluent family and did well with your studies, you were set for a life on the building sites or the greenhouses. This was the real thing at this school at this time, those that did well academically were encouraged and nurtured, normally these were the same individuals that came from prominent families and affluent areas such as Swanland and Ferriby. If you came from a council house, you had no chance, if you came from a single parent family or there was any signs of abuse or neglect at home, it was ignored and put down on paper as a disruptive child. For obvious reason I absolutely hated school, in fact towards the end I only went in for my dinner, it was the only meal I got that day.

Chapter Three- Satan Donivon

I think it must've been summer in 1991 and I was at Brough crossroads with a friend from school called Paul Milner. Both of us were rockers however Paul's Mum would not allow him to grow his hair long but his record collection was quite impressive including Poison, Mötley Crew and Aerosmith. However, Paul's ultimate group was the LA group, Vixen.

It must've been about half past ten on a Saturday night, when a car pulled up at the crossroads and inside were Jimmy Crisp driving and a lad that was a few years older than me called Joss. I knew Joss well and in later years we would become very close friends, however I did not know Jimmy at all other than his sister was friends with my sister at school.

"Now then Joss, how's it going mate?" I can't remember what Joss' response was but to fill you in a bit more about Joss he was six foot five, skinny as a lamppost and had hair down to his ass. He was also a few years older than me at school and it was well known his favourite group was Iron Maiden. Iron Maiden badges were all over his jacket as well as the obligatory Iron Maiden tattoos. Joss was also a target for the school bullies in his year, constantly the dickheads in Brough that were trying to keep up with the spoilt rich kids of Ferriby and Swanland would often make Joss' life a misery in school, not only that, the teachers targeted Joss as well, again he had long hair and he was tall, which meant he stood out.

As soon as Joss got out the car and Jimmy followed, we all sparked up a cigarette each but it was Jimmy that spoke first. "You've got a sister called Nicola, she's friends with my sister Gillian" then he added " I also hear you want to join a band. If you set me up with your Sister, I'll let you join my band as a singer." That was the first time I met Mr. Crisp and although I agreed in theory, I made it clear it wasn't up to me whether my sister would want to go out with him or not. Jimmy was also going out with a girl called Danielle at the time from my year. Jimmy, like Joss, was a few years older than me and came from an affluent family, even if it was very dysfunctional. Jim lived in the shed at the bottom of his Dad's garden, commonly referred to as the wash house. Inside the wash house was a single bed, a sink and a partitioned off toilet. Also, there was a TV and video and on top of that loads of music equipment including guitars, amplifiers, a drum machine, microphones and a PA. The only thing that was missing from the wash house, was a proper drum kit, however there would have been no room.

The conversation carried on that night at the Brough crossroads and maybe there was some magic in the air. Within an hour, all four of us went back to the washhouse and I had my first audition as a singer for my first ever group. Initially, it was agreed that I would be the singer for Jimmy's band with Joss on bass but Jimmy wanted to hear me sing first. I must admit, at first I was nervous and I could not sing, that was until I started doing a James Hetfield of Metallica impression, put in a bit of gruff on my voice. Joss, Jimmy and I agreed I would be the singer, this was the start of my time playing music in bands and being creative.

It was later agreed that our first proper rehearsal would be on the Monday in the wash house. At the time, I was living with my friend as things were difficult at home, I clearly remember Jimmy turning up early to pick me up, he was that keen that we start making music, also whilst at school any thought of any academic qualifications went right out the window. I wasn't interested in school in one iota. I would however, spend the days in lessons relentlessly writing songs. Just about every song I wrote would be material for the group. The first song I wrote was called "Lost war song" and I also wrote all the others.

We also struggled for a name for the band, initially it was going to be called 'The Freaking Witches' however this was the name of Joss and Jimmy's group long before I joined. In the end, whist watching "Top of the pop's" one night and enduring a Jason Donivon performance and remarking how shit he was, Jimmy came up with the name 'Satan Donivon' and this name stuck throughout the life of the group.

There was still various things we hadn't achieved yet, not to say we were not hard workers, because we worked religiously. Our practice regime was five days a week. Monday, Tuesday, Thursday we worked from half past six to half past ten then Friday and Saturday from ten PM until two in the morning. This work schedule went on for three years. It would only be later that it would all turn to shit.

The general regime of the practices was the following. We'd get to the practice on time, there was no excuses if you was late. We'd run through the whole set of songs, then we would work on new material, quick tea break and a smoke and end the night going through the whole set of songs again. The routine was good for the band and it was certainly good for me as a young teenager, as it gave me some purpose when things were going to shit at home.

One evening when Joss and I turned up for rehearsal, things had changed, some might say, changed for the worse. Jimmy had a girlfriend called Danielle, I'm not going to say too much about her, however Danielle decided she needed to be at every practice. Not good, look at The Beatles. It wasn't perfect, but Joss and I made do because after all, even though I wrote all the songs or at least most of them, it was still Jimmy's band.

Another occasion was Christmas eve, we turned up to rehearse, at the wash house, when Jimmy let us in and said "It's Christmas eve, we're having a night off, we're going to watch "Silence of the Lambs" and get pissed." With that, Jimmy got out two twelve packs of larger and we spent the night and early hours basically letting our hair down. With Danielle there, of course.

The one thing we had never done, although we had talked about it a lot, was gigs. We had discussions about doing a gig at South Hunsley school, also a fellow group that we knew well were called The Septic's and they'd gigged at the club "Adelphi" several times. The "Adelphi" as it is today, is a grass roots venue and many bands starting out had played there over the years including Shed Seven, Happy Mondays and it's claimed Oasis played there too in 1993.

As far as gigs went, we had no experience but it was decided, mainly by Jimmy, that we would take things to the next level once both Danielle and me left school. There was one problem, Danielle was now pregnant at this point.

As I mentioned above, a group we close with, was called The Septic's, this included my best friend from school, Chris Boodie on bass guitar along with his mate Stew, who was a few years older and his mate Andy. Again, like Satan Donivan, The Septic's used a drum machine. One Saturday evening, at rehearsal, for some reason it was just me and Jimmy, Joss was working away in Leeds and God knows where Danielle was. Jimmy decided we would pop to The Septic's to see if they fancied a jam with us at the wash house. Both Stew and Chris lived in Ferriby and both were happy to pop to ours. All in all, it was a really good night of jamming with your contemporaries. Jimmy had always been in awe of Stew as a guitarist and to be fair, Stew was quite a player, taking influences from groups like Slayer, Suicidal Tendencies and a big influence was Kirk Hammett from Metallica. We hung out and jammed for hours and it must've been six o'clock in the morning before we finished. We even manged to rework a Satan Donivon song called "Lost War". Obviously, Joss was not too pleased that he had missed out, especially as Chris had been playing bass that night, maybe he even felt threatened. However I was absolutely positive that Satan Donivon were going to do something, maybe over confident, it would soon all turn to shit.

The last days of school approached. Of course I'd been expelled at this point along with Chris, however we were both allowed to return to take our exams. I clearly remember standing outside the school gates on the last day, along with Chris and a few other undesirables that were my mates and watching the school buses take the rest of the year home. We waved to some of them and I clearly remember watching Sally Lambert blow me a kiss from the bus, this is the girl that took my virginity on a school trip to Rotterdam, despite the fact she was going out with a kid called Jonathan Hoskins at the time, I wasn't bothered he was a bit of a lad because he was also a dickhead. All the time on my last day of school, I could not wait to get stuck in to making music with the group.

Two days before, I was at practice and again Joss was away. There was however a slightly dark kid at our rehearsal called Steve Burton. Burton went to the same school as me and Joss, only slightly older. In fact I think he was in Joss' year. There was however, no love loss between Burton and Joss. At the time I didn't understand why. Burton and Jimmy seemed to get on very well and I must admit at that point, I quite liked the guy, he seemed to be like another muso to hang out with. He was funny, shared his fags and like us, a bit of a bad boy. He was also a singer.

Anyways, leaving school, I was pleased to be out of the place. No more authoritarian teachers making life hard, it also meant leaving behind what were known to me and Joss as 'The jocks', these were the posh kids that were into sport and did very well academically, also these were the ones the girls always went for, in other words spoilt rich kids. It was a relief to get away from the place.

Two days after leaving school, Jimmy turned up at my house. I clearly remember my sister letting him in. I didn't think out of it at the time, however he came in and his words were " I've got some bad news, the band has broken up." I did not take it in, I was stunned, I asked him to repeat it. Again Jimmy said " The band has broken up." Then he added "Danielle is in the car, we are going to go shopping in town, do you want to come?" It was so nonchalant and I could not believe it, the whole band had worked so hard over the last three years for Jimmy just to dismiss all our efforts. Again I challenged Jimmy " What about Joss? What has Joss said about all this?", Jimmy looked sheepish, then added "I don't know, I've not seen him." Then as quickly as he had arrived, Jimmy turned and said "Anyways, Danielle is in the car I've got to go."

My whole world was shattered in the two minutes that Jimmy had entered my house. Within a few days, it became apparent what had happened. The fact was Jimmy had no intention of doing anything with the band, he just wanted to make music in the wash house, the other factor was Jimmy was making a lot of money working as a plumber at his dad's company, not to mention Danielle had now a little boy at this point. The night I met Steve Burton and thought he was a stand-up guy, was the night that Jimmy and Burton plotted the downfall of Satan Donivan. Burton was in a band but they needed a lead guitarist and a bass player and Burton always had Jimmy's ear. From what I can gather, Burton said to Jimmy "Sack Robbo from the group and you and Joss can come and join our band." And that's basically what happened. Satan Donivan was no more.

Chapter Four- Influence

So here I was out of school, a singer with no band and still trying to learn to play guitar so I could be the next Eddie Van Halan. With the dramas and chaos at home, it wasn't long before I moved out and got my own place on Newland Avenue, along with the thirty five pounds a week YTS course that was supposed to support me. Around this time, I was hanging out in night clubs a lot including Romeo and Juliet's (just before it got shut down by the police), Quidleys and of course Hull's famous Spiders. One of the key mates I hung out with was Lee Bailey. We'd met at the green houses several years earlier, when we was both working as labourers picking tomatoes. It was a hard and thankless job. But it kept me out of trouble during the school holidays. Also, with Lee was his girlfriend Paula and Lee's best mate Dodsy. One thing we all had in common was, we were all rockers. We also all liked to party. This included drink and drugs. Lee had been at me for a while to join his group, Influence, as a singer and every time I told him I was doing things with Satan Donivan. The difference between Influence and Satan Donivan was Influence had a drummer. However, both were similar in styles and heavily inspired by Metallica as well as Pantera.

Lee basically got me on a bad day, whilst I was sat in my damp, one-bedroom bedsit on Newland Avenue. I agreed to be the singer in his band Influence, however to be honest working with Lee was better on paper than it was in practice. I met his band and on lead guitar was Jamie, he was roughly the same age as me, about seventeen. Lee was on the bass and by all accounts he was very good, then there was the drummer, quite a bit older, maybe twenty seven, his name was Phil and he lived on Bransholme.

Initially, we all got on very well, we would go to Quidleys and hang out and try and impress the rock chicks by telling them we was playing in a group (I should mention at this point Lee and Paula were finished) However there was one fault with the group, the fault was Influence were shit also the drummer Phil was the owner of the most amazing bright white Yamaha drum kit, this included double bass drums and Zildjian cymbals. Phil certainly had the gear and it had cost him a fortune. If memory serves me correctly, he had paid over three thousand pounds for it, which in 1993 was a deposit on a house. The only problem we had, Phil knew as much about playing the drums as I know about basket weaving in Tibet. Phil could not play the drums to save his life, even though he had the most amazing Lars Ulrich drum kit. The fact Phil could not play was lost on Jamie and Lee especially as Lee and him had become quite close. However it was not lost on me that Phil could not play and Phil knew it.

Influence would rehearse as often as we could and this usually meant a Saturday in a rehearsal space off Hawthorn Avenue in Hull, this space has long since been demolished. Also, Influence's song writing was crap, Jamie and Lee both wanted to be the song writers and were addiment that I couldn't contribute. But the lyrics they wanted me to sing went along the lines of " Misconception of your mind, inflicts torture on your soul.". Also they had a thing about writing about warlock and mountains and again you could see where groups like Metallica and Pantera's song writing were a key component. Lastly, in between playing at far too high a pitch, a drummer that could not keep time and everyone spliffed up between songs. Ultimately, it was a far cry from the discipline of Satan Donivon and quickly I lost interest and this was also picked up by the group.

The other thing that was apparent at this time, I was always listening to different forms of music, not just metal and again this was sacrilege to the lads in Influence, for some reason they though it should only be Slayer or Napalm Death, the heaver end of metal. It wasn't long before tempers start to fray and on top of this I was struggling with my mental health for the first time and could not properly communicate as a result. Then one night I was at Lee Bailey's house when I ended up getting off with his little sister, nothing too serious just a kiss and a fumble as we walked the dog but the mistake I made was I told Jamie, who couldn't wait to tell Lee the singer had copped off with his sister. The last time I saw Jamie he turned up at my bedsit wanting to borrow an album, begrudgingly I lent him it and then he turned tricks.

When Lee found out I'd copped off with his little sister he was livid. To be fair it wasn't like she was in nursery, she was only a couple of years younger than me, however Lee was having none of it, Influence then all decided that if they were going to support Megadeath on tour, that I would not be the singer to do it and to be honest I could not care less once they'd sacked me. We'd achieved nothing, no recordings, no gigs, no support slots, just two or three good nights out. If the truth be told, the only one of them that could play was Lee, Jamie was okay on guitar and liked to think he was a bit of virtuoso but he was nothing compared to how good Jimmy Crisp was in Satan Donivon, as for Phil, the drummer, he is the only drummer I know that knocks three times on the door and comes in late (Drummer joke).

So again, here I was, a singer without a group and guitarist that could not play. On top of this I was living on my own in a bedsit, that I could not afford and working in a YTS garage, in a job that I could not stand. The next band was just around the corner but would that work out too?

Chapter Five- Sens

Lee Nixon or to use his nickname, Nicko, had been a good friend of mine for a lot of years. When I hung around in Hessle, he was the first kid I met that was also a rocker. Nicko was into groups like

Pretty boy Floyd, Poison, Mötley Crew, however one night when we were all having a smoke in his bedroom, I had a copy of Nivana's "Nevermind" on cassette, which I lent Nicko and never got back. From this point on, Nicko absolutely loved Nivana and I must admit this album sounded great when you'd had a smoke.

Nicko had been mates with a couple of brothers off his estate called

Mathew and Andrew Foster and again I think Nicko introduced them to Nivana. It wasn't long before Nicko formed his own band along with Mathew and Andrew (Guitar and drums) on bass was a kid we knew called Louie, again he was another kid off the estate. I was still determined to be the new Eddie Van Halen and I approached Nicko to see if I could join his group on guitar. Again, because Nicko and I had been real good mates, he was happy for me to join the group that he called Sens. There was however one problem, there was already another guitarist auditioning for the role. Chairman had also grown up in Hessle and not only this, he was higher up the food chain with the other guys in the group.

I first met Chairman at Hessle police station. At the time my Mam was working as a Lawyer and asked me to meet her at the police station so she could take me home. I'd been in Hessle all that afternoon and Mam just happened to be at Hessle nick. I'm not quite sure if Mam was representing John, however as I waited in reception, John came in after being released from cells. He quickly saw me and sat down next to me. Now I knew John from sight, and he obviously knew me, however I wasn't sure of his name other than when I remembered about a year before, Nicko and a few of us were having a smoke and then we walked into Hessle square when a couple of lads came out around our age and John was one of them. They had all been at John's house drinking and John, being John downed a full litre bottle of vodka in the space of an hour and was so hammered he could hardly walk and with these lads was now laid out in the street throwing up violently. Whist we were in the chippy, we'd got the lady on the counter to ring him an ambulance, but I distinctly remember asking her to get our chips first. We then sat with John asking him if he wanted a patty and chips whilst we all waited for the ambulance to come and take him to get his stomach pumped.

So, while we were sat in Hessle police station John and I got chatting about groups and guitars and bands, at which point John told me he was in a group and that they were called Sens. It wasn't the easiest of conversations to hear and it soon became apparent that if I wanted to be in Sens then Sens were going to have to choose either John or me.

The other kids in Sens included Andrew and Matthew, by all accounts I knew straight away that Andrew was a good drummer and the whole band would rehearse in the spare room of Andrew and Matthews's mum and dad's house. Matthew was quite a dedicated guitarist, and I distinctly remember neither Andrew or Matthew were particularly bothered about the drugs scene, the party scene or even getting a record deal. It was more about playing their instruments for the fun of it.

What I should say over the years Andrew and Matthew both became like brothers to me. Having said that, at the time and of course, John Chairman was picked as the guitarist. Again, I was gutted. And I must admit, slightly jealous of John. I thought John was a bit of a non-entity, also I felt I had more experience in groups and knew more about bands and so I was very green that John had been picked. In hindsight, John also did what he was told to do. Also in hindsight, it wasn't really Nicko's group, it was more Matthew and Andrew's.

 What I would say is, despite my best endeavors, I still could not figure out or get my head around playing guitar. This was regardless of how many hours or how many lessons I had. Even something as simple as tuning went right over my head and to be honest it was little wonder John was picked over me, it still hurt though. I was about seventeen, without a group, without a gang, no prospects and also this is about the time when my mental health deteriorated so much, I had a mental breakdown in Hessle square and very soon after ended up in a Psychiatric hospital for the first time.

Sens continued with various line ups including Joss, my old bass player from Satan Donivon. Also Jimmy joined for a short spell, however I do not want to write too much as this was never my group, what I would say is that for the next five or six years Andrew, Matthew and myself were inseparable and I witnessed all the lineup changes including when they got a female singer called Jill of whom I was smitten at that time. But like I say, Sens was not my group, I was more of a Sens groupie. Every weekend Sens would play a gig somewhere and I would often go and get drunk, jump in the van for a lift and end up stopping either at Matthew's or with Andrew and his partner at the time, Tanya.

Other groups on the scene at this time, around 1993, included Prime Risk, the name was well suited as they used to do a lot of Gary Glitter covers, long before everything came out. Another group which were well established on the Hull circuit, were God's Medicine. God's Medicine at the time were untouchable and without a doubt the biggest group in Hull. They had a massive following and to be honest, massive egos. However they were primed for big things. Years later, God's Medicine would often turn up at Matthew's flat on Victoria Dock after Sens and Medicine had finished gigging and party the night away. The difference being, Medicine would bring drugs and there was always some groupie that came to the flat, if anything it was almost like we was in awe of them. Another reason they came to Matthew's flat was because of Moody, who happened to be the cousin of the two guitarists Grey and Webo.

Chapter Six- A Change In The Water

Something was about to change as we approached 1994. It would involve two brothers from Manchester called Noel and Liam. They were called Oasis. Initially, when I first heard Oasis I thought they were nothing compared to bands like Led Zepplin or Van Halan or even AC/DC, however like all good groups, they grew on me. Not only that, they began to grow on the whole country, Oasis were definitely a break from the traditional.

Nivana were finished at this point and it was like there was a void. Then there would be programs on TV like TFI Friday and I distinctly remember Noal Gallager being interviewed over Easter weekend and they asked him about burglaries in Manchester before they started the band with Noah just saying "No comment" and it getting a great laugh.

The thing about Oasis was they were different, people could relate to them, they were the kids we grew up with on our streets, they spoke about what we knew and what our lives were like and ultimately they did not care who they offended. By Noel's own admission, " The press can write what they want about us, we don't care, as long as they put us on the front cover." A new generation of groups had taken over and at the helm were Noel and Liam Galliger. Even in the years to come, I always thought Oasis were a bit like the great groups of our time, even in the years after Oasis were in their height, I'm not going to name these groups but I tended to feel they were a poor man's Oasis. Nothing ever topped them.

Another thing that happened around this time, Andrew and I were looking through the window of Goth and Davy and there was drum kit for sale without cymbals for roughly three hundred quid. Andrew and I had talked a few times about me playing drums, I'd even asked my Mother to get me a set at Christmas and again she was addiment, I was not having a drum set in the house. The thing was even in the early days of Sens, Andrew would leave his drumkit in my bedsit and I would often come home from my crappy garage job and figure out drum pattens for AC/DC songs. I was surprised how easily I picked it up. The other fact was, my Dad was a drummer and many times on the road I would see him knock out rhythms on his steering wheel whilst listening to groups such as Deep Purple, Gary Moore, U2 and others.

Many moons before Mum and Dad got divorced, Dad came home pissed up from Welton club one day and took me to his friends Laurence Arnent's house. Laurence was a drummer that knew my Dad and he had invited Dad round that afternoon to go on his new drum kit, Dad took me with him and I was allowed to go on Laurence's kit and again, I took to it quite well, even Laurence commenting at how quickly I'd picked it up. I would have been about seven or eight at this time.

Fast forward to 1994 and Andrew and I are looking at this percussion plus drum kit. Andrew just turned to me and said " Why don't you go in and make them an offer?" Which I duly did. Within half an hour I was out of the shop and I had agreed to pay them fifty pounds a fortnight until it was paid in full out of my dole money. We agreed once the final payment had been made I could pick up my new drum kit. This began a whole new chapter in my life. I was no longer a wannabe guitarist, I was now a drummer.

I wouldn't say I'd mastered the drum kit at this stage, but I could hold a rhythm and keep time. One day I get a phone call from a kid called Ronnie. He was putting a band together and they rehearsed at the Ferryboat Inn, on Hessle Foreshore on a Sunday. I was interested and I got Mum to drop me off. At the time, it was very much a part of the Brit pop scene, however I cannot remember what songs we went through. What I can remember is a mate of ours called Pierce being the singer. Pierce would later come into my life as an outstanding nurse at the Humber center when I was sectioned. Back then though, he was a lad off our estate. All the group were good lads, but unfortunately nothing ever came of it, not even the name of the sed group.

Later down the line, I got another call. Again, it was a group needing a drummer and they did a mixture of covers and some originals. They weren't bad kids, but they were just not my type of people. Okay, they were from Hessle, however most, if not all of them, went to a private school. It was almost like a load of posh kids trying to make out it was important to be working class. The songs were okay, but I just knew playing in a group was a stop gap for these guys. Almost like a year out before they went to university to become an accountant or a lawyer. Unlike the bands I'd been around, all these guys had their own cars and posh cars at that. All paid for by Mummy and Daddy. Like I said, they were not bad guys, but I felt I had nothing in common with them. After hanging around with Sens for all them years, if the van broke down, then we had to fix it. Sometimes, the tires would be running bare. There was an authenticity to what we were doing. This new group didn't seem to get that. We did a couple of gigs at the Adelphi, then I decided to leave, not only because I didn't feel comfortable, but I also missed playing with my own.

Chapter Seven- Mike Foster group

Andrew and Matthew were gigging regularly with their group Sens. Matthew had a flat on Victoria Dock at this point and Mike Moody was now living with him as his flat mate. Sens had access to their own studio on New Cleveland street and it wasn't unheard of for us to fire up the gear at ten o'clock at night only to finish at six o'clock in the morning, go back to Victoria Dock and listen to whatever recording we had made.

Around this time, things were happening in the Sens camp, which might have meant cancelling gigs around Hull. On one of these late night sessions myself, Mike Moody, Andrew and Matthew would get together, thrash out a load of covers in order to cover the gigs that Sens were not able too. There was two Mikes and two Fosters, hence the Mike Foster group. It was my first time working with Moody and as mates we all gelled very well, musically and with our sense of humor. We went through covers such as Elvis Presley's, "Buring love", Bowie's "Space Odessey", the usual crowd pleasers like The Kinks "You Really Got Me" and "All Day and All of the Night", basically our repertoire was more old classics from the sixties to the late eighties.

Unfortunately, for various reasons, the Mike Foster group never did anything more than the odd dodgy recording on cassette (Remember them?) and several rehearsals. I can't particularly remember for what reason we never gigged, however Mike had his own thing going on with his solo career and both Andrew and Matthew were both extremely busy, not only with Sens but other groups on the circuit wanted them also to fill in here and there.

The experience I got stayed with me and I was more confident playing in a group environment.

Chapter Eight- Dirty Deeds

Around 1996, I'd put an advert up in Goth and Davy, along the lines of "Drummer seeks band", also I'd seen an advert for a bass player that was into the same stuff, AC/DC, Metallica, Status Quo, Black Sabath, Ozzy etc. His name was Steve. I rang him and he lived right up East Hull and at the time I lived in Brough, one of the West Hull villages. We had a quick chat on the phone and I decided I'd pop up and see him. It took me two hours to cycle to his house. As soon as we met, we clicked. Steve had literally just left the navy, he wasn't into drugs, he loved classic rock and the cherry on top was he could play bass guitar very well. Within half an hour of meeting Steve, I just said "You're in".

Within a couple of weeks, we had a singer called Paul, a lead guitarist called Joe, a rhythm guitarist called Lee as well as Steve and myself. We would rehearse once a week at studio 46, going through classic rock numbers. After an hour and a half, we would go across the road to the Odeon cinema and get a drink in the bar. This gave us a chance to get to know each other better, decide what songs we wanted to do next and generally shoot the shit. There was a problem however, I didn't particularly take to Paul, also Joe hardly ever learnt the songs. I didn't dislike Paul, but he was however a special policeman and I got the impression he wanted leadership of the group. Later down the line, I would often refer to him as "Policeman Paul". Again with Joe, the fact that he failed to learn the songs, would often leave a bitter taste in my mouth and occasionally I would lose my temper. Some of the songs Joe failed to learn, were songs that he had picked. We did however have a name for the group, all of us fans of AC/DC, we picked the name "Dirty Deeds" after the song.

One of the main gigging pubs in Hull at the time, was Spring Head. It was a large venue and once a week, I think on a Wednesday, they used to do an open mic, where groups or friends could get up and perform a couple of numbers. I thought it would be a good idea before we booked any gigs that we perform at the open mic. It was a good opportunity for us to bond live, without the pressure of a paid gig. The other thing, it was an opportunity for the friends and family of the group to find out what we had been doing for that past three months.

Paul and Joe were particularly nervous, whereas Lee and Steve were more relaxed and I was just up for it. We got up and did "Hell Ain't a Bad Place to Be" and "She sells sanctuary" and by all accounts we did a good job. The crowd loved us and generally everyone we brought to Spring Head, got on. However, with the power struggle between Paul and myself becoming more apparent and the griping with Joe, I decided I would leave Dirty Deeds. Probably much to the delight of Paul, whom as soon as I left decided that he wanted to sack Lee and change the name of the group. The only one who tried to get me to stay was Steve and I distinctly remember him chatting to my Mum, trying to get me to change my mind. Steve and I remain great mates up until this day. He's played in several groups and is currently the bass player in a Status Quo tribute act. Steve also, because he was such a good mate, was an usher at my wedding. We don't see each other all the time, but both of us know, were only a phone call away from each other. As for Lee, years later we would come to work together again.

As far as Spring Head goes, it won music pub of the year in the late nineties, which became a bit of a poison challis. After they won recognition, all of a sudden the price of the beer went up, they started charging people on the door, even on open mic night and generally the place went downhill. Even to this day, it's not the Spring Head it was in the nineties.

New chapter Nine - Rock goes to college

Around 1998, Hull college had a new course starting around musical theatre and live performance. It was Barry, Matt and Andy's dad, that encouraged us all to enlist and initially we all did. College then was at the Riley center off Anlaby road, this is now a housing estate. I remember the first day of term in September and we went in the performance hall, was all made to stand in a circle and introduce ourselves to each other.

Talk about misfits and outcasts. I can't remember the names of everyone I went to college with but I seem to remember one guy who was a great singer/songwriter and had a very 'Jim Morrison' thing about him, however even though he was younger than me, he was a complete piss artist. I remember one day this guy saying "Come on we'll go down Hessle Road, I know a couple of slags that'll buy us drinks all day." That was one of the guys at college. Another was a big camp guy called big gay Dan. He later went on to appear in Big Brother in the noughties, but has since disappeared into the insignificance.

Then, most memorable of all, Andrew and I were walking back to the Riley center when this guy from college came up to us, we'll call him Derek, as were walking back to college Derek, a mixture of new age hippy and classic rocker, and as I remember at the time he was sleeping in his dad's shed, anyways Derek approached us and was obviously stressed about something. " What's been said? What's been said?" Andrew and I just looked at each other wondering what on earth was going on. In the end, we said "Look Derek, we don't know what the fuck you're going on about." And then added "What's happened mate?" he just responded and said " There's been a bit of a hoopla." As he finished he walked off dejected.

Andrew and I are none the wiser and we walk into college were everyone is sat gossiping, and I happened to mention we'd just seen Derek and asked what happened. Of course everyone went quiet. It was only later we learnt Derek had followed one of the girls into one of the recording rooms, thinking he was in, lowered his trousers, got his cock out and asked her if "she'd like a bit of this." In hindsight, when he said there had been a bit of a hoopla, he wasn't fucking wrong. What we should've said " Oh you mean you got your cock out for Lisa?" Obviously Derek was thrown off the course. We never saw him again.

Initially there was a good banter between everyone that was on the course, even some of the acting students got on well with the musos. Especially in the run up towards Christmas. The college were putting on a pantomime, the actors were to star and sing in it and the muso were the backing group. I can't remember what the play was, but we had to learn a mixture of songs and it was the first time I got to play in what you might consider a professional environment. Generally, after the end of every performance, all the students would go round the town. This included some of the tutors. One of the tutors, who I won't name, would often take the odd student to bed after a night out. The next day he would play it down while he stood outside the rehearsal block with a cup of tea and a joint.

After Christmas things got a bit tetchy. All I wanted to do was perform and play the drums but, there was the academic side which none of the musos seemed to take seriously. This included our Matthew. The upshot was, just about everybody on the course failed. Plus it seemed to me that the student actors and the musos weren't getting on as well as they did. It started to get to the point whenever there was a performance, that the actors wanted to play as well as perform and as far as I was concerned, this wasn't their job. The whole point of the muso's course was for us to play our instruments, but the actors didn't see it this way, to be honest it all got a bit bitchy, particularly amongst the camp actors. To add insult to injury, around this time I'd stopped taking my schizophrenic medication, therefore I wasn't functioning on all cylinders. By the end of the semester, Andrew had left, Mike left and both Matthew and I had failed the course. To be fair I wasn't that bothered and it was only Matthew that went back the following year. In the end our Matthew did four years in total and qualified.

New Chapter Ten- Jonny Cortina and The Big Ends

After college and after I got well, I spent a bit of time in the Parachute Regiment in Pudsey. Not that it's relevant to this book, other than it got me fit and I did not pass P Company. Later down the line I joined Prince of Wales own Regiment, passed out and won most improved recruit. Later down the line, I tried joining the SAS. In between being away with the regiment, I was still knocking around with Matthew and Andrew, I'd also got my first proper flat at this point, a proper bachelor love nest.

A few months into moving into my new flat, I got a phone call from a guy calling himself Willow, Willow was looking for a drummer for his new project. He was an older guy in his late fifties, he had long grey hair and looked a bit like Robert Plant. He'd definitely been on the circuit and around the block a few times. At the time Willow was living in a flat in Ferriby. When I first went down to meet him, his partner answered the door and he was in the living room smoking a joint. Both Willow and I got on very well. Well into the formation of the band, he would tell me stories about himself. Willow was once in the British Army Intelligence Core, however, when the military didn't work out, he packed his bags and made his way to London to make his name as a musician. Over the years he had done several jobs, some legal and some illegal. Mainly he had worked around the music scene and I remember him telling me when back in the sixties he was looking to do a group similar to early Pink Floyd, that was until he saw and heard Led Zepplin for the first time and like he said, everyone realized they were doing it wrong and that Led Zepplin was doing it right.

Another interesting story, about Willow's past, he had been all over the world at various points, either as a roadie or a musician. Even playing Knebworth at one point. But the one story that stood out the most. Willow was friends with a Columbian drug dealer, we'll call him Eric and Eric was into lots of things, including making porn films. Willow happened to be at one of the productions when the male lead had 'Stage fright' should we say, therefore Willow stepped up as the role of the performer, including wearing a bus conductors uniform.

Willow gave me a list of songs to learn, most of which I had no idea what they were, they were defiantly all blues numbers from the sixties, including songs by Chris Farlow and other sixties numbers. I can't remember who else was in the group, except we had an exceptionally good blues guitarist and a flamboyant singer. After several rehearsals, we had our first gig at the Polar Bear. I can't remember how much we got paid, but I specifically remember Willow complaining that they were earning the same money in the sixties and seventies and that over the last thirty years, it had hardly gone up.

It was my first proper gig and I wondered how I would get on. I walked into the venue at seven P.M on a Saturday, along with my drum kit and started to get set up. I think there must have been a football match on at the time, because at the bar was a pissed up guy in his forties, maybe ex-military and he was watching the football. The minute I played a beat on my drums he kicked off, " Start playing them drums while the football is on, they'll be going straight out the window" I was just about to respond by saying "If you touch my fucking drums I'll break your nose" when Willow stepped in and said " Robbo just hang fire for half an hour, when the footballs finished, we'll set up." All in all, the gig in Polar Bear went well that night. We was even re-booked, which was not bad for our first gig. I also remember, a few of the lads came to see us play including Kipper and Steve from Sons of the desert, Steve from Dirty Deeds as well as Matthew and Andrew.

As a first gig, we got off to a running start, however we had a gig at Sportsman, on Hedon Road, one night, which ended in a mass brawl. We'd got there early and got set up, had the sound check and was ready to go for nine. Initially, it was a good atmosphere, the punters were enjoying the songs and back in them days Sportsman always got busy. It was around the time that Pam and Dave Grundy ran the pub. Towards the end of the night and we were firing down, we was on our first encore when all of a sudden in the crowd, at the front of the stage, two blokes started scrapping. It was like blue touch paper on a firework, because within half a minute, the whole pub was scrapping. One half of the pub trying to fill in the other half, like two forces of nature. In the middle, was a seventy year old Dave Grundy punching anyone that stood in his way. I should also say, my Dad and Dave Grundy were good mates in the seventies and Dad would tell me that Grundy was a hard man. I must admit in his seventies, he still had it, as I watched him floor several people to the ground.

Within about half an hour, the fight had ended and the bar staff were cleaning up the glass that was on the floor, we got paid and made our way home but it was a learning curve and one where I realized that it didn't matter where you was gigging, any venue had the potential for it to kick off at any moment.

Around the September and I had been called away by the Regiment, nothing top secret, just a two week exercise in Scotland. I remember I got back late on the Saturday night and as a result, of running up and down hills in Scotland for two weeks, I slept in Sunday morning, when we should have been rehearsing for the group. Willow was not happy, the guitarist was that livid he'd left, because he had left, the singer had left also. End of the Jonny Cortina and the Big Ends.

Chapter Eleven- The New Retros Part One

Andrew at this point, was working for Kings beds, whom had a big warehouse in the center of Hull. It was an ideal practice room.

One night by chance, Andrew arranged for a jam. Mike Moody was singing, on bass was Steve, from Sons of the dessert (Andrew was the fulltime drummer for Son's at this point) and lastly who should be on guitar and rhythm guitar, non-only than Mike Moody's cousins Grey and Webo, the original members from God's medicine. This was no mean feat and I must admit given the presence and impact that Medicine had in Hull, it was a great coup to have a couple of Hull's most successful musicians, I don't mind telling you I was in awe.

We all seemed to gel quite well musically, we did a few Who numbers and just jammed anything that we all knew. This was particularly good for me as a drummer because it meant I only needed to know patterns, not chords. Things were about to progress from there.

Initially, we did not have a name, also Steve from Son's could not commit, therefore Mike bought in his mate Rich to play bass. I distinctly remember the first practice at Rich's flat on Spring Bank. There was Grey and Webo, myself, Rich and Mike Moody. To be fair, we all knew Rich as Mike's mate anyways, we all got set up and both Rich and Mike were having a fag and then started arguing over the ashtray. At this point Webo piped up, " Come on lads, how can we go to parties with Paul Weller and Coutney Love if you're going to sit there arguing over ash trays?" It was the sense of humor that Webo bought to the band and it would go well beyond The New

Retros.

Webo and Grey had both broken up with their partners at this point and were living together on the Avenues. It was a proper bachelor pad and it was a joy to pop in at any hour for a coffee. Whenever I went round, there would be different music from different eras blasting out. In fact, I think it was Grey who introduced me to a group called Dr Feelgood, particularly Wilko Johnson. However, both the brothers had a certain respect for all types of music. That house in the avenues was where I got my musical education. Both Grey and Webo introduced me to Aretha Franklin, Marvin Gaye, The Jam, The faces, The Who and Creedence Clearwater Revival. Nothing was off limits. Obviously there were some things I just didn't get, mainly around punk, or more specifically underground punk. Also, I wasn't over keen on some of the Ska tracks that they would play, however that's the joy of loving music.

Grey and Webo were great intellectuals. Their knowledge of history, in particular Military history, was something a university professor would be jealous of. Both knew things about my Regiment and my Regiment's history that I did not even know. Also, both brothers did not have a problem with my schizophrenia. Every time something was mentioned, either Grey or Webo would refer to Kieth Moon or Spike Milligan. It wasn't that they had an in depth knowledge of mental illness, it was more an empathetic attitude that wasn't a problem for either of the brothers. This was long before it became fashionable.

One of the most empowering things about working with Grey and Webo, was their attitude to my playing. Often, when working out songs I would get a feel for the rhythm then ask, "Do you want this drum pattern or that drum pattern?" with Grey and Webo, it was more of a case of you're the drummer, do what feels right. In other bands I'd worked in, usually the singer or lead guitarist would be telling me what they wanted me to play. As a drummer this can be frustrating. The New Retros, it was more of a punk attitude, in the sense, the song goes like this, learn it and play it.

The other thing, any fills, roles or cymbals I wanted to put in, I was free to do it at my own discretion, no one had a problem with it, it just had to sound good. Playing with this attitude was great for me, it meant I had my own freedom to do what I wanted. I would not tell Grey what solo to play in the same sense, he did not tell me how to play the drums. Everyone was responsible for their own instrument.

Grey and Webo also had some fantastic stories to tell. Early on into their career, they were gigging with a band called Sidewinder. Sidewinder were playing at the old tower ballroom, as part of a talent competition. At the time, Grey played a red Stratocaster and the Compère picked up on this. The compère was trying his best to be a cheeky chappy and in the evening on stage, while Sidewinder were being interviewed, the compère turned to Grey and said "Is that Hank Marvin's guitar." At which point Grey responded, down the microphone, in front of everyone "Nah mate, got it from Argos." The compère's face was a picture and everyone cried with laughter.

On one occasion, when they were gigging with God's Medicine, a girl turned up whom knew the band. Her and her boyfriend had been following Medicine for some time. However, on this particular evening they'd have a row. She stayed with the band and watched them all night and at the end of the evening she was a bit worse for wear, therefore Medicine offered to drive her home. Stopping at the garage to get fuel, that used to be near Hull Royal Infirmary, one of the lads opened the side door to get the money to pay for the fuel and once the door was wide open, in full view of the four court, this girl was being spit roasted by the drummer and the bass player. It was only later they learned that she got back with her boyfriend and eventually they got married.

Another tale they told me was about a mate of theirs, who ended up as part of a road crew for a group called Killing Joke. Killing Joke were big in the eighties and sort of a bi-product of punk. The story goes, they were at some celebrity shin dig, might have even been top of the pops, when who should come along, but eighties legends, Bananarama. Even though Bananarama at the time were bigger than

Killing Joke, they were all huge fans. However, as the story goes, Bananarama were also the biggest slags in music. Every one of them got nailed by Killing Joke that night. (Waiting for the lawsuit. Behind the band- The book that Bananarama wanted to ban.)

Lastly, Webo told me about a group he was in, when the Bass player and his girlfriend decided to have a threesome with his best mate. Thing were going great until the two blokes fell out during the act. Then started punching each other and scraping, whilst all the time the girlfriend was in between both men.

It wasn't long before we was out and gigging. Grey decided the name of the group was to be "The New Retros". The only difference being, Mike was not very good at the banter or talking between songs and this is where Grey and Webo stepped up to the mark. Both brothers had been working the circuits for years, even playing up and down the country, therefore both were very comfortable on stage. It showed in our performance that the sense of humor that Grey and Webo bought to the stage and interacting with the crowd, basically this is where I learnt my stage craft.

More than this though, Grey was a fantastic guitarist to play with, I could see how his style was very angry, to the point and pure. I'd played with some great guitarists at this point, not least, our Matthew, however Grey was in a league of his own when it came to improvisation.

I never knew where Grey was going with something, but I always knew where it would end, if that makes sense. No two night Grey played the same thing, was it because Grey was good with the group or was it because I was developing as a drummer? Also, I should mention, I was still very much involved with the Army and I was extremely fit, as well as in my mid-twenties. If I wasn't away with the regiment, on any gig day, which was normally a Saturday, I would go to the gym, run ten miles on the running machine, in the space of about two hours. This would get me ready for the gig on the night and loosen me up. I also remember listening to a lot of Paul

Weller's drummer (Steve White), early Van Halan drumming and a lot of Deep Purple records, seeing what I could copy on stage at the gig, therefore as a drummer, I was probably at my peak at this point.

One gig I remember clearly, was the night Elton John, played Hull's new football stadium. We was gigging at Griffin (a venue made famous by The Beautiful South, as it was their watering hole). It was a great atmosphere, all the songs were going down really well and the place was banging. Webo, however, had forgotten to take his medication for his epilepsy. We was nearly at the end of the night and doing a great rendition of "Gloria" by Van Morrison, all of a sudden, with less than three songs to go, Webo collapsed on stage. I didn't know what was going on at first, I thought it was part of the act. Then I looked down and saw Webo's legs shaking and at this point I'm thinking maybe he's been electrocuted. I jump off my kit and make straight for the phone at the bar, at that point I'm ringing an ambulance, I'm also thinking had Webo took something? The gig was well and truly over and it was hard work getting an ambulance.

Grey came into his own. "Robbo, Webo doesn't need an ambulance, he just needs to get home and get to sleep." I tried arguing with Grey, that it was best all round if he went to hospital and Grey's response was " Robbo, he's my brother, I know exactly what to do." In all fairness, I couldn't argue with that. A mutual friend called Binge took Grey and Webo back to the Avenues and me and Rich packed down.

To add insult to injury, the guy who had the Griffin at the time, agreed to pay us on the condition, the next gig we did there was free. Grey had booked three gigs in with the guy, so he had us over a barrel. In the end, all's well that ends well, first thing next morning, I went straight to Grey and Webo's and the only injury Webo had was his pride.

Chapter Twelve- The New Retros Part Two

There were however, tensions in the band after a while. I had a very military attitude, in the sense that nothing was impossible, if we put the effort in. Grey and Webo on the other hand, not only were they contending with their breakups, they were used to doing things in a totally different way. One problem we had was our photoshoot. At the time I knew a guy who was a keen photographer. We all chipped in and agreed to pay him to do a photoshoot at mates rates. We all got dressed up, early the Saturday morning and I remember wearing my best suit. There was however, a problem, Grey, being a mod, he wanted me to wear a tie. I flatly refused, I was sure I looked smart. Grey decided then because I wasn't wearing a tie, he wasn't getting his photograph taken. It ended up with a band shoot with no Grey, it was a real shame because the photographs that came out were brilliant. Grey, like me, was a perfectionist. If it wasn't right for him, then he would not be doing it.

Then we had problems with Moody. We'd have a gig booked in for months, then all of a sudden, Moody would ring Webo and say his voice had gone, only for us to find out that on the date of the sed gig, Mike's agent would ring him and ask him to play somewhere else, which Mike would do, because it meant he had more money for himself. In Mike's thinking, Why do a gig for two hundred quid, split five ways between the band, when he could earn eighty to one hundred pounds doing a solo gig. It was a very self-centered and selfish attitude. Ultimately, this would lead to Mike's downfall.

Later into The New Retros and Mike wanted a new PA, only he wanted the band to pay for it. He managed to persuade everyone, except me, that the gig money should go towards Mike's PA. Webo and Grey managed to talk Mike round and explain to him that Robbo's the drummer, he doesn't even use the PA, why should he pay towards it? The rest of us will put our gig money towards it. Initially, Mike said he was fine with this, however he wasn't, within half an hour he was at my house, telling me the band had decided that he was getting the gig money for a PA, at which point I rang Webo and told him I'd left the group. Both Grey and Webo were furious with Mike. I'm not 100% sure what happened after that, but soon after I returned to The New Retros as they recruited a new singer called Colin.

Colin was a weird character. A bit younger than me and had never done any gigs before, but I must admit his voice was pretty cool. His image was that of a young Jim Morrison and he was not 100% confident as a singer. He also had an attractive girlfriend who was a teacher and they had a little girl together. Initially, I got on well with Colin, he tried hard and he looked like he deserved to be there. There was however, problems with Colin too.

Our first gig with Colin as the singer was the Griffin pub. Colin was nervous to say the least, a bit like a rabbit in the headlights. We all did our best to look after him, however during the first set, I had to pick him up on the fact he kept turning his back on the audience. We finished the first set and Colin was livid, he didn't like the way I'd spoken to him and was threatening to walk out, it was only Webo and Grey that managed to calm him down. In the end, he finished the gig.

A few more gigs under our belt and Colin was growing more confident, it was only then we realized why. Before every gig Colin would take a full box of ProPlus and half a box of headache pills before washing it all down with a pint of Stella. At one gig, in Hessle, on the day of Hessle Feast, the gig was going well but Colin was on another planet. At the end of the gig we all packed down. I put my drums in a Vauxhall Astra I had at the time, whilst the rest of the boys, including Colin, got in Rich's campervan with the gear.

About an hour later I get a call from Webo. "Robbo, We're sacking Colin, he's a dickhead." I didn't know what to think and I certainly didn't know what had happened. I made my way back to the avenues to Grey and Webo's, to find out what had happened. When I got there, the whole band was in agreement that Colin was no more. Turns out, Rich's girlfriend was in the van along with the group, making their way back, when Colin and Rich's girlfriend started arguing. From what I can gather, it was an argument over nothing, but Colin was very much off his head. By the time the group got to the Avenues, Colin had jumped out, said he was leaving the group and walked down the street shouting " Wankers, Wankers" like he was seven years old.

To replace the singer was one thing, however we had gigs booked, which we had to honor. After hearing the group's side of the story, I made my way to Colin's flat. It took him twenty minutes to open the door and he was that paranoid, he thought I'd come to fill him in. In his hand was a boiling hot cup of coffee that his girlfriend had just made him and in front of me, he pulled up the sleeve of his shirt and poured the hot coffee over his wrist. I could see the steam coming off his skin, yes there's no doubt about it, Colin was a poorly bunny. In the end, I drove him up to Brantingham Dale to calm him down, walked him up the hill and he seemed to calm down a bit. Crisis averted, however it was only for a short time.

One of the places we used to rehearse, was the Malbrough Club on the Avenues. It was a great venue, however it is now flats. Because the owners used to let us rehearse there, in return every couple of months, we'd throw them a gig. I remember the gig clearly because it was a Sunday and I was away with the Regiment. Fortunately, I got finished early and managed to get to the club on time. Colin and the barmaid were getting on famously, so much so that at the end of the gig he went back to hers, bearing in mind, Colin had a girlfriend and had a weak mind. We all told him "Colin don't say anything to your lass about you sleeping with the barmaid." In fact, we could not drill it into him enough. Taking into account, we're a rock and roll band and things happen and basically, what happens on tour, stays on tour. What did Colin do? Went straight back to his girlfriend and told her he'd slept with the barmaid. Colin's relationship with sed girlfriend lasted two hours after that. Within a month, Colin had left The New Retros and had a breakdown during a gig. After that, back came Moody. I never found out what happened to Colin after that.

Chapter Thirteen- Sons of the Desert

I was starting to make my name as a drummer around the town. Our Andrew's band "Sons of the desert" called me out of the blue one Saturday morning. Not to go into too much detail, but Steve the band leader, asked me if I would step in that night at the Sportsman. I knew playing for Sons of the desert was a big deal, at the time they were probably the biggest band in Hull and certainly most established. I managed to get a lift with my drums to the venue, well before the band got there. Also, I had my suit on. I'd seen Sons several times and again the soul influence was paramount. They did songs like "Superstition" by Stevie Wonder, also James Brown numbers and Blues Brothers covers.

I had to have my game face on. The other things about Son's of the Desert, Kipper, the front man, is the finest front man in Hull as far as I'm concerned. There was nobody who had a better voice or was sharper with the banter. On one occasion, Son's were playing a pub called Kingfisher, off Anlaby Road. As you can imagine, it was rough as fuck. In between the numbers, a pissed up thug shouted "Play some fucking Jonny Cash" Kipper sharp as a tack, responded " In a minute Mam."

Other banter Kipper had been known for, nearly got him in trouble. Doing "I feel good" by James Brown, and at the end of the song, Kipper said to the audience " That was a James Brown number and I'm not going to condone the fact that James Brown used to batter his wife" then straight after he said, " Then again she properly have deserved it." The response was magic and there was a shameful laughter from the audience.

All in all, the gig went well at Sportsman. The guitarist, Dave, took me and my drums back home. I was however, a bit disappointed that I didn't get invited back for a drink at Steve and Lou's for the after party. Playing with the Son's of the Desert, was a different league and it was a privilege to do it. Later down the line, when I got married, Kipper played my wedding in his new group, Soul Patrol.

And again, Kipper was on point and it was a fantastic show and a fantastic day.

Around about this time, say around 2004/2005, I was to have my own nervous problems. My career in the Military was going really well, that was until I put myself forward to join the SAS. Cutting a long story short, I failed selection due to hypothermia in the Bracken Beacons. As a result the MoD looked into my medical records and found I'd lied on the medical to get in. After an investigation, I was kicked out of the Regiment, Christmas eve, 2004. The last words the CO said to me, " We can have you in Robinson, if you're not on your medication." This lead to a whole different chapter in my life. Some of you may be aware, in 2016, I published a book on Amazon Kindle called "Sectioned- The book the NHS tried to ban." This explains more about what happened at that time, feel free to buy it and if it's any good, leave a review. In short I'd stopped taking my medication, got sent to prison for common assault, got put on escape charge in prison, moved to a secure unit, which I broke out of, whilst on prison transfer and as a result got given an indefinite hospital order and I spent the next three years in the Humber Centre.

Chapter Fourteen -Sectioned

Life in the Humber Centre was not fun. For the first six months, I tended to read and stare at four walls. Later down the line, I got moved to a different ward and as a result, there was more activities to do. One of the activities was music. Paul was the name of the occupational therapist and I must admit even though he was a bit whacky, he was top draw when it came to keeping you busy.

One day, Paul approached me and told me he had been given some funding to buy some instruments, including a drum kit. Paul also asked me would I be interested in doing some music with him. I didn't have to be asked twice. More than that, I even told Paul where the best place was to buy sed instruments. At the time, there was a shop in Doncaster called Electro music, it was the old fashioned music shop that you don't get anymore. Everywhere in the shop were guitars, drums, PA's and every other type of instrument you could think of. Obviously, there was a lot of second hand equipment, however the deals at Electro were fantastic. Even to this day, I have a pearl export drum kit that I part-exchanged to Electro, for a bag of shit percussion plus.

Paul took on board what I had said about going to Doncaster to get all the equipment with the grant. Within a week, he had returned with a drum kit, bass guitars, lead guitars and singing equipment such as a PA. First thing Paul asked me to do was put the drum kit together. Soon after that, it was a case of finding guys from the wards that were happy to start a band. To be fair, we were quite fortunate.

Will from the wards thought he'd pop down to see what all the fuss was about. First thing I showed him was how to play "Paranoid", by Black Sabbath on the bass. To be fair, Will picked it up pretty much straight away. Then there was Luke, he was a nice kid, although a bit misguided. He was however, well into his music. He said he would sing. That left me on the drums and Paul, the OT, on lead guitar.

Nobody in the group knew what they were doing, except me. To cut a long story short, I found I could lead the group into what they needed to do. I sort of became the group leader, and the name of the group was to be called Sectioned. Over a period of a few months, we learned about four or five songs. This may not sound like a lot however, some days not all the band could make it. This might be down to leave, day release, tribunals, hospital appointments or even staff shortages. Paul however, worked really hard, literally learning all the songs in his spare time. I think he was a secret rock star in an OT's body.

One day Paul said "Right guys, I've got an idea. Why don't we do a gig in the canteen, for the hospital." Everyone was up for it, however I was the only one that wasn't nervous, after all, I'd been gigging for some time now.

On the day of the gig, everyone was like a rabbit in the headlights, except me. Paul had this idea that he wanted to dress us up, also he wanted us to use makeup like kiss. He had even bought four plastic wigs. We got set up in the canteen just after dinner and I had to explain to everyone " Look If you miss a note, don't worry about it, nobody will hear it." I added " The other thing to remember, if you mess up, just find out where you are in the song and pick it up from there." An hour before showtime and Paul made us all wear wigs, however I drew the line at wearing makeup. We had four songs to perform, although I cannot remember what the other three where, but we opened up with "Paranoid". We performed in front of a few of the patients and a handful of the staff.

Generally speaking, it went well. Even members of staff were coming up to me, telling me what a great drummer I was and they didn't realize I could play. This was the only gig we ever did as Sectioned. I was due to be released soon, therefore I had a lot of leave. Also Luke, got moved to Leeds. As for Will, I don't think he realized how much potential and opportunity he had to continue as a bass player. Good bass players are like rocking horse shit on the circuit, they're so hard to find. It was obvious he was musical and he picked up the bass quite easily. However, he was also due to release soon and wasn't interested in continuing.

Life in the Humber Center carried on for another six months and I was eventually released on the first of July, 2009. Lastly, I should add, I cannot thank the people enough that visited, phoned and supported me during this time. Matthew came regularly, also Steve from Son's visited, Jill from Sens rang me regularly as well as writing to me, Webo and Mike came regularly and I had a fantastic support from the majority of my musical family. If you read sectioned, you'll know I was very fortunate to have all the support I did, not least from my own family and a few friends from the army.

Chapter Fourteen- The Fixers Part One

After I was released from the Humber Center, I returned to my rented house on De La Pole Avenue and as I'd mentioned, a lot of my musical family had kept me in their life during my incarceration. This also included Joss, who had come to my house for tea, this particular evening in late August. We'd mentioned about putting a band together for some time. We'd talked about doing classic rock covers, obviously Joss on bass and me on drums. We'd even had a practice a couple of times with a kid from Grimsby on lead guitar, however this went nowhere as towards the end, this guy would cancel an hour before practice, with some stupid excuse.

At the time, I had a dog called McNab and I just so happened to be taking him for his evening walk, whilst Joss was doing the pots, when my mobile rang and it was Webo. " Robbo, how do you fancy doing a band with me and Moody?" I was well up for it. Also I mentioned to Webo, Joss was at mine and he was a bass player, that used to be in Sens. Within an hour, all four of us were sat at Webo's, talking about what songs we would cover. We did however need a lead guitarist. As luck would have it, I had been to Goth and Davy's in town that day and had the number of a guitar player. What I did not realize, till I made the call, was the guitarist happened to be Lee from Dirty Deeds. Within the space of an hour, after Lee had arrived, the Fixers were born.

Initially, we would practice every Thursday at Webo's house, this usually meant acoustic guitars, I would play bongo also there were masses amounts of booze and weed. It became a bit of a working piss up, but the songs were forming. Again though, there was a problem with Moody. I won't go into too much detail, however it was decided by the rest of the fixers, that Moody wasn't going to cut it, therefore, Webo would do the singing until we found a replacement.

The piss up turned into proper rehearsals. On a Tuesday, we would rehearse at Webo's, acoustically whatever the new songs were, then on a Thursday, we would go to the Rehearsal rooms and thrash it out live. We did this for around four to six months, when I started touting for work. I remember our first gig was at the Polar bear on an open mic night. I wanted us, particularly Lee, to get used to playing live together without the pressure of a paid gig. Everyone came to see us that night. Jill was there from Sens, our Matthew, our Andrew and a lot of our long term friends came to support us.

Doing gigs for free is a great starter for bands and groups. However, if you do too many people will take the piss. On this occasion, I wanted us to do a gig for charity at an open air fate. The fate would take place in the villages in East Hull on the way to Withernsea. It wasn't like anything I'd expected it to be. It was a mixture of who's got the shiniest tractor and The Wicker Man. This village was literally in the sticks and their must've been about ten miles from our turn off. The villagers themselves were lovely, however they were extremely religious. We got set up and waited for our turn and we sat on the grass as a group, again with some of our mates.

Over the microphone was a lady and she started talking about Jesus. On and on she went about how through Jesus' love God gave us a robin and the robin has wings and Jesus loves us because of the robin, also she mentioned because of Jesus' love, he gave us butterflies that fly in the spring and pollinate the farms. At the point Joss, who had always been a Pagan, indiscreetly as he could said " Fucked a right pig last night." Then Joss decided to continue, " Worst blowjob I ever had!"

Both me and Webo had to say to Joss to cool it. It wouldn't be so bad but there was kids running round as well. We did the gig, I think a few farmers got up and danced, we got packed down but for some reason, we never got re-booked and never got asked back.

Down the line, I got our first paid gig at Highland Laddie off Southcoates Lane. Again, all our friends came to support us, however the money was atrocious. I'd basically blagged the landlord that we would do a cheap gig for him, if we could play, I think we got about a hundred and thirty quid. The night went really well, although it wasn't packed by any means. Webo came into his own as a front man as well as doing rhythm guitar and just about every song went well, including the obligatory "Mustang Sally" at the end of the night. It was probably Lee's first gig and he could not believe that he got paid even though the money was terrible.

The landlord asked to re-book us, but I said the money had to go up. The landlord refused, so that was the end of that. This wasn't a problem for me, as I had plenty of time on my hands, even though I just started at college. When not at college or at rehearsal, I would spend my day driving around the area, including Hull, Beverly, the villages, etc, touting for work. Also, I'd got in touch with a couple of agencies. The work started coming in gradually and more and more we was gigging every weekend. On top of this, the money started to improve. For the likes of me, Webo and Lee, the money made hell of a difference.

One of the gigs we started playing at regularly, was the Salthouse Taven, on Salthouse lane. Even though it was a bit of a foodie pub, it wasn't a bad venue to play. One night, after we got set up, Webo and Joss spotted a couple of attractive girls in the bar. Being red blooded males, went over to try their luck and by all accounts, got on really well. In hindsight, I think one was blonde, one was brunette, both late twenties, early thirties. Initially, they said they was only having a drink with a meal and they were soon going, however we must have been playing well as they decided to stay and have another bottle of wine. Webo even said down the microphone, to one of the girls "This next song is for you, It's called 'Feel like making love', by Bad Company." In return this girl gave him a look, as if to say he was in. We were just about to finish at the end of the night, probably on the last song, when one of the girls made a b line for the toilet. Soon after her friend followed. As we started to pack down, Webo and Joss went to look for their female company. At that point, I spotted them both coming out the ladies toilet, one smiled at me, then they both made straight for the door. Joss and Webo's conquests had left them. It was only when we was packing down, we realized what had happened. The girl who made for the toilet initially, must've had something that didn't agree with her and as a result shit all over the bathroom floor. At this point, her mate must've realized there was something wrong and helped her tidy herself up. Then they had to escape without anyone noticing. But like the song says, sometimes you think you're going to get it, but you don't and that the way it goes.

Soon, I'd moved back to Hessle. Generally, after every gig, we would all pile back to either mine or Webo's and put the world to rights. Towards the end, I always made sure I had plenty of drink in, therefore everyone would pile to mine and it wasn't unusual for us to be shooting the shit till five or six o'clock in the morning after gigs. We had some amazing talks and nothing was off the table, from politics, religion, music, women and sex.

Joss wasn't the only one who could be inappropriate. Lee came into his element a few times as well. On one occasion, we'd gone to see Webo play in his other band, Reflector. Reflector was a group Webo did with Grey, however they didn't gig as often as The Fixers. At the time Lee was seeing a black girl Krista, Lee had always had a thing for black women, however Krista was from Africa somewhere and had moved across from Huddersfield to be with Lee.

Both Webo and Grey's girlfriends were at the Reflector gig and they both were asking Lee about his current girlfriend. Lee was happy to oblige in the conversation, then he asked if they wanted to see a picture. Then out pops his phone and shows the girls a lovely picture of Krista laid on the bed, naked with her cat hanging out. Fortunately, both Grey and Webo's girlfriends found it funny, however sometimes it felt like the band I was in, were not of planet Earth.

The Fixer's had been playing for a good year at this point and during one of our after gig, late night discussions, Webo got talking about the Navy and in particular, Portsmouth, the home of the Royal Navy.

I'd mentioned a few times that my Mother was from that part of the world and I still had family there.

One afternoon I had a call from down south, it was a social club that my cousin and uncle both went to regularly. They both heard that I was playing in a band and put in a good word for us at the club. The club booked us for the Sunday night on the August bank holiday. Not only was the money right, it also gave the band an excuse to go on tour. I agreed with the club that we would play but it would depend of whether I could get other gigs in the area that weekend.

One Friday night, Julie and I and my Mother went for dinner early in the evening and for some reason I was restless. I decided then and there that after dinner Julie and I would drive to Portsmouth, stay in the Navy club and book a load of gigs for the next bank holiday.

The trip in itself was successful. I'd blagged three gigs in Gosport, next to Portsmouth and this included the social club. All I had to do now was get the accommodation. There was a bed and breakfast at the bottom of my Uncle's street and I booked us all in for the August bank holiday. Webo's Brother, Eggy, was also up for coming on the trip as well as our Andrew. There would be three cars going, sleeping two to a room.

The night before I could not sleep so I decided not to fight it and left for Gosport at about four in the morning, just me and my drums. I had text Andrew as he was driving and also Joss to meet me there. I arrived with plenty of time to kill so I just got my head down in the car. At about six o'clock that evening, our Andrew turned up with Lee and Eggy, then half an hour later, Joss and Webo. We didn't have time for long hellos as we had half an hour to get to the first gig. Arriving at the venue, the bar staff looked like they had no idea we was playing, even though our posters were up. The gig itself was pretty mediocre. There wasn't a big crowd, although the ones that were in enjoyed it. At the end of the night, the bar manager came up and said "How much do you want?" I told him and he didn't seem phased about it.

The next day was a Saturday and we had the whole day to explore. Walking down to the Gosport ferry, we passed a music shop. Webo saw a PA that he absolutely needed. I'm not sure what PA it was but it was cheap in the scheme of things. He borrowed some money of Eggy as well as using all of his own money, the upshot was the idea of us exploring the dock yards in Portsmouth went out the window because Webo couldn't afford it. This was starting to piss me off. The whole idea of going to Portsmouth was to explore the history. I started to bite my lip and I wasn't the only one, in fact during the whole trip, the only one that didn't piss and moan was Lee. Joss would spend every minute in his room, stalking his then girlfriend on Facebook and complaining about whatever was in his head. Andrew disappeared a couple of times and turned up two minutes before the gig. All in all, you learn a lot about your band when you go on the road with them.

The second gig was at a pub again, just down the road from my Uncle's house. This time the venue was packed full of young kids. Everyone seemed to be enjoying the tunes. There was even a couple out celebrating their anniversary. We got chatting to this couple and towards the end of the night, both of them were pretty pissed. Then, the bloke got up on stage, grabbed Webo's mic and proclaimed to the audience we were the greatest band he'd ever seen and we really had made their anniversary something they would remember forever.

Later, when we were packing down, a couple of these young kids were giving Eggy death stares until they realized he was with us. Then they turned their attention to an old guy, I seem to remember he was in a wheelchair. I kept saying to him, "Who's giving you a hard time? Also they're not going to mess with me, I'm from Hull." In the end I got Eggy and Andrew to walk him home.

The last gig we did was at the social club. As social clubs go, it was fairly busy for a Sunday night, but not packed. It was a funny sort of crowd, they half loved you and wanted to be your friend, and they half wanted to be up on the stage doing it themselves. I had a AC/DC t-shirt on at that gig, which was picked up by one of the old ladies in the crowd. She went onto say her daughter and son in law plus three of her grandkids had recently had photos taken, all wearing AC/DC t-shirts. It was a great story and at the time we did an AC/DC number. We decided we would dedicate this song to this Granny. However, because we did not tell the crowd the full story, she kicked off like fuck. Like I said, a funny audience.

At the end of the gig, they adrenaline was flowing with all of us. Therefore, I decided we would drive back that night to Hull. Also, Joss' car was playing up. I did not want Joss to have to deal with that during rush hour, if it broke down. So it made sense to drive home.

There was an argument or discrepancy about money. The fact was, we had none. It had all gone on our digs and fuel. We made absolutely nothing on that outing. This lead to an argument between me and Webo on a petrol forecourt at about 2 o'clock in the morning at Fareham. Even the forecourt attendant shouted down the microphone, that if we didn't behave she was going to call the police. All in all, the experience of touring as a band was great, however, at this point I'm the leader of the group and so all the managerial things were down to me, as a result, a bit like having four girlfriends at the same time, no one is every happy and everyone wants different things.

One night we did a gig in the Norland in Hessle. It wasn't a bad gig by any means, in fact Webo managed to pull a bird. To try and be a great wing man, I took Webo and this bird home via Asda where they could get a bottle of wine, then dropped them off and left them to it. Joss and Lee helped pack down, then let themselves in my house. We all started talking about the nights gig, when Lee spoke up and said Webo wasn't a great singer. Few more drinks later and we started to talk about it some more. It wasn't long before we all agreed, we needed a fulltime singer. I knew this was going to cause problems and I also knew it would be down to me to tell Webo, "We're looking for a singer." I must add, at no point where we thinking about getting rid of Webo. Webo was far too important, not only as a rhythm guitarist and could work the crowd, but as a band mate. Still, I wasn't looking forward to the phone call.

Chapter Fifteen -The Fixers Part Two

I was right about the phone call to Webo. He wasn't happy. First he blamed me and surmised that I'd set it up with the band the minute he pulled a groupie and was out the picture. This was very much not the case. If anything it was Lee that had suggested it, then Joss agreed, therefore there was not much I could say or do, other than take the consequences.

About a week later he had calmed down and rang me not only to apologies, but to go along with the plan. The plan was we would put the feelers out for a new singer on social media and in the music shops. I seem to remember Joss also put something on Facebook.

It wasn't long before we had responses. One guy rang me and he was an alcoholic, so he was no good. Then there was a guy who wanted to join the band whom was already out gigging as a solo artist and a karaoke king. I really didn't want the same scenario we had with Moody, where a gig would be booked, only for our singer to decide to tell us he was ill and gig somewhere else for more money. Again, he was no good.

In the end, three guys were in the running. We'd booked a rehearsal room at Robbie's on Hedon Road, from there each of the three singers were given four songs to learn, then allocated a time to come to the rehearsal room. The reason I'd gave them four songs to learn for rehearsal, was simple. If they could not learn four songs, which wasn't a lot, how would they be able to learn a set list. If memory serves me correct, the songs were "Shaking all over", "Substitute", a song by the Hives and another. I'd purposely picked four different genres just to see if they could learn songs they didn't necessarily like or listen to.

At Robbie's we'd got all our gear set up and ready to go, when I got the first call. The first singer rang me with some bullshit excuse, that he could not make it. That was fine, he was dropped, the reason being, if he can't make a rehearsal, how can he make a gig? An hour later, the second singer arrived, to be fair, he did quite well. He wasn't a party animal, you could tell that and he had learned three songs well. The only one he struggled with was the Hives, it was obvious he didn't like it. I must admit, Joss and I were keen.

Then the third singer came, his name was Ian. I wasn't sure about Ian at first, okay he could sing the songs, but he drove a pimped up Ford Fiesta. Not only this, during the rehearsal, it was transpired he was a football hooligan for one of the Hull City firms. His voice was quite strong though, especially the Hives number. Ian even went out of his way to learn the other three songs, so that meant he wasn't biased about anything he had to sing. Half an hour later and Ian had done his audition and went. Lee and Webo wanted Ian, however, Joss and I wanted the other guy.

Again, as was becoming the routine, words were said. It was reluctantly agreed we would try the first guy. Again there was a problem, I rang him to say he had the job, only to learn he couldn't make all the rehearsals and some of the gigs because he was a solo act and some of the dates clashed. That was him finished, we had no choice, we all had to go with Ian. I rang him half an hour later and told him, if he wanted the job he could have it, however he would need to get his own PA, also no drinking and drugs at practice or gigs. Ian seemed quite pleased and promised to get his own PA, which he never did. In the meantime, we just used Webo's PA.

I felt it important to gently coax Ian into singing by doing an open mic night at The Rider Club. It would take the pressure off a full paid gig, also it would get him used to playing with a band in front of an audience, as well as, the band getting used to him as our singer.

The first night at Rider Club cameand Ian was as good as gold. There was however a problem with Joss. His girlfriend at the time didn't want him to gig. Cut a long story short, our Andrew stepped in on bass.

Generally speaking, Ian was a natural. He had the arrogance of a singer and his persona was very street. We had to tell him off a couple of times for swearing down the mic, however this was his first gig and he wasn't to know the etiquette. The etiquette was no swearing down the microphone, particularly depending on what venue you was in, however, if you can read the room and think you can get away with it, that's one thing. If not, don't do it.

Another example is the likes of Liam Gallager can swear down the microphone, the only difference is Liam Gallager sells out stadiums, he's not just another pub singer. Other than that, Ian did really well. After the gig, we all had a few beers at mine. It was only later down the line, problems with Ian would arise.

The whole dynamic of the group had changed. Ian had bought a certain amount of credibility with him, having said this, some of the guys he bought to the gigs were less than desirable, generally football hooligans and low level drug dealers. The Fixers as a band were getting tighter as musicians, the whole buzz of the group was we enjoyed playing live.

The gigs were coming in thick and fast at this point. The general consensus was we would gig on a weekend, then generally during the week I would go gig hunting. This consisted of finding a date and finding a venue and generally making sure we were booked full every weekend. The more we gigged, the tighter we became.

If it was a bank holiday, generally we could gig at the minimum, three times that weekend. Another idea Webo had, probably from experience, was to print laminated post cards of The Fixers. When going to the venue to tout for gigs, we would drop a postcard off, then generally whoever was behind the bar would pop it into the gig book. That way if a group cancelled, our flyers would be the first thing they saw when looking for a replacement. The other advantage of this, when a venue rang us, or usually me, desperate for a band, I could charge what I liked, within reason.

Some of the gigs that were of note, was Half Way on Hessle Road. At the time Sophie and Wayne ran it and it was a well-run pub with no bother at all. Often, when setting up my drums, I would let Sophie and Wayne's lad, who would have been around six or seven at the time, have a blast on my kit. Generally, nobody went on my drum kit, except our Andrew. I would often joke with Sophie and Wayne that the lad was a natural and I would help them get a drum kit for Christmas, however for some reason they didn't quite think it was a good idea.

It was a summer's evening at The Halfway and there had been a funeral. Everyone was in black and the atmosphere was moody. Once we got up and started playing the atmosphere turned on its head. The whole room seemed to light up and just about everybody was having a good night up and dancing. Back then, Halfway used to host a swingers night, so towards the end of the gig, I asked down the microphone " Who was here for the swingers night then?" at which point a couple of drunk girls in the audience shouted they were. I responded by saying " So is your sex on fire then?" and we broke into the Kings of Leon number. The whole roof nearly came off. Towards the end of the night, we had three cheers for the guy whose funeral it was and this also went down very well, although his name escapes me. Of course, on the back of that gig, we got rebooked several times.

Another gig that came to mind, was Priory, on Priory Road. Initially, we'd been booked in for Five Ways pub that night, however when I got to Five Ways and started setting up my drums, a miserable cow from behind the bar said " What are you doing?" I went onto explain that we were booked in and I was just setting up. In response she told me she was the new Land lady, also she knew nothing about us and we were not playing.

Generally, I would take the posters in three weeks before the gig, whilst there I would confirm the booking. In response this miserable cow just said "The old Landlord told me nothing about it and we don't need a band tonight." As frustrating as it was, I had to think on my feet. I packed down and rang around the group, then told them to rendezvous at Webo's house. In the meantime, I went looking for another venue. To me it seemed pointless not to play when we was all fired up and ready to go. He other thing, half the band were on the rock and roll, therefore we needed the money. I walked into Priory about half an hour later and spoke to the Landlord.

Basically I came to an agreement, we would play tonight for free, in return if we was any good we would have a free drink each as well as a booking. The night was a complete success although, initially when we was setting up, the Landlord looked like he didn't know what he had let himself in for. For all he knew, we might be a black death metal group that would empty his pub. As the same as Halfway, we took the roof off the Priory that night. Not only did we get several bookings, we also got New year's eve, which was always a good payer. All it took was for me to use my initiative not to waste a gig.

Even though the gigs were cracking, it was still down to Webo and myself to do a lot of the banter. This wasn't a bad thing and it took the pressure off Ian. Like all singers starting out in groups, they're the center of attention, this can be a good thing or a bad thing. If something goes wrong, everyone looks at the singer, as Ian was still new to the game and not quite mastered stage craft, Webo and I tended to do a lot of the jokes and talking between songs. Later down the line, I think Ian resented this slightly as he wasn't the center of attention when it was going well. Also the truth be told, Webo and I probably got comfortable being in the limelight and taking some of the attention from Ian.

Again, as it was early on in Ian's introduction to the band, I would often book charity gigs. I'm a big believer that if you do a gig for charity, you do it for free, if not don't do it. A lot of the bands I know are ruthless bastards and will do a charity gig but even if it's a reduced rate, would still want paying and expenses. To my mind, this takes away from the charity, which defeats the whole object. Even to this day, it's concept I've taken with me. Love him or hate him, Burnard Manning used to say the same thing. He would point out about cheeky chappies that were family friendly, would have a persona that they're friends to everyone whilst at the same time, fucking the charity out of whatever money they could get.

Don't get me wrong, you can spend your whole life being a charity act. People will always want you for this cause or that cause, also parties, birthdays and weddings, people will ask you to play for free. What they fail to realize is, guitar strings and drum sticks cost money. Also, rehearsal rooms and studio time costs money. Not to mention, the hours perfecting your craft, whether that's learning your instrument or a song, or perfecting the sound as a group. The general consensus I have, I will do a gig for free, but maybe no more than three or four a year. Also, it has to be a charity that's close to the bands heart. In our case it was military charities, mental health charities and seafarers charities.

One night, a girl rang me that was raising money for a cancer charity, she asked if I would help. She'd hired a hall in East Hull and was hoping to do a ladies night. The twist in the tale was she was also an Ann Summers agent. I agreed that The Fixers would play, much to the moan and groans of Webo and Joss.

We arrived at the venue, at that point I told the band there was a catch. We would also be modelling some of the Ann Summers men's briefs. Initially everyone in the band was up for it, I certainly didn't mind getting my kit off in front of a load of women. Webo on the other hand stayed quiet. Into the evening and there was a drag act and a load of male strippers that looked like cheap versions of Arnold Schwarzenegger. Not a lot of money was raised that night as there were very few ladies that came. I wasn't bothered, I was still looking forward to getting my kit off, Webo, however said he wasn't doing it, that meant Joss spoke up and said he didn't want to do it and of course Lee went along with Webo also. To be fair to the girl who'd organized it, she said it wasn't a problem as she was going to get the male strippers to do it. Also, because there were so few in, she invited us to pack down after the first set. It was a bit of a wet squid, but we'd done our bit for that night. I never did get chance to get my kit off though.

Another thing that I was keen on, bearing in mind I'm running the band at this point, this meant I sorted out the gigs, the practices, the money, the posters, just about everything, however I was keen to get more exposure. This meant doing talent trail. Talent trail was a competition run by Hull Daily Mail. In particular, Webo and Joss did not want to do it. From past experience, they felt bands never won it and it was always a waste of time. I felt different. Even if we got through to the semi-finals, our name would be in the paper at least twice. This in turn meant people would have heard of The Fixers. As a result, I pushed for it.

There was a venue down Anlaby Road, called Brownies. This was the venue for the first heat. Of course, most of the band were just not up for it, probably down to Webo and Joss' moaning. Anyways, I pressed on and we got up and did three songs, all of which I felt went pretty well and I was sure we would get through to the semi-finals, especially given the competition.

The other thing I felt we had going for us, we were the only group of the night, the rest were karaoke kings or singer/songwriters. After we'd finished our set, three young girls got up, all must've been late teens, early twenties. As for the clothes they wore, they looked like they were all from Bend Over movies, in fact if there miniskirts were any shorter, you could have seen what they had for breakfast.

They got up and did their thing and even though they had no stage craft, sang a couple of songs and blew kisses to the judges. Of course they got through. The Fixers, however did not, and I was livid. There was not one act that was on that night that was better than us. I even went up to the judges and had a go at them, I went on and told them they voted on tits and arse over real musicians. One of the organizers that night was Vicky Norman from the Hull Daily Mail and even she told me to wind my neck in.

Things were to take another turn that night as well, whilst Joss was outside having a cig, he was chatting to a couple of guys. Joss went on about how bands never win Talent Trail, when one guy said a group called the Costello's won it last year. At which point, Joss opened his mouth without thinking and said "Yeah but the Costello's suck cock." This might not have been so bad however, the bass player from the Costello's was sat next to him and took great offence. On it went on social media that night the Costello's and The Fixers had a beef with each other and it was there for everyone to see. I knew nothing about this until our Matthew rang me the next day and told me what was all over Facebook.

The only good thing from Talent Trail that year for us was that it got our name in the paper, other than that, we had lost to a load of dancing prostitutes and had a fall out on social media with another band. Later down the line however, the singer from the Costello's would end up joining Webo and Joss. What he probably wasn't told, since the fall out on social media, at every venue The Fixers played and during the crowd participation, we would say "Can we have a big boo for the Costello's." Down the microphone. The reaction was priceless.

Chapter Sixteen- The Fixers Part Three

Things seemed to be going well for The Fixers and the general rule after every gig was the band would pile back to mine, get pissed and put the world to rights. I must admit in the early days this was fun. Drunken conversations till early hours in the morning, talking about everything and anything, nothing was off the table. From politics to religion to music to bands, all the time we'd have a classic album on in the background. These albums may include Aerosmith's "Toys in the attic", The Faces "A nod is as good as a wink in the blind house", "Rumors" by Fleetwood Mac and we constantly would listen to the Rolling Stones back catalogue. And I particularly remember the song "Tumbling Dice".

These were the fun times, we bonded as a group and we bonded as musicians. However most important of all we bonded as mates who became brothers. Unfortunately for us though, this was not to last. With at least half the band, being out of their heads on something, it wasn't long before arguments and cracks started to appear.

At first the arguments seemed light and were soon forgotten, but then ego's started getting in the mix along with cheap amphetamine, the arguments got more and more severe when we were all supposed to be winding down after a show. Some of the things that were said were quite cruel and I was as bad as anyone for this. It was getting to the stage where the after show party became more of an after show therapy or after show argument. Like I said, more than half the group were off their tits, which I felt meant they could not rationalize any point of view or an argument properly. But then this is rock and roll. When does anyone say "He's turned into such a nice lad since he's been taking cocaine." I'd always said I wasn't bothered what drugs the band took, as long as it wasn't in rehearsal time or on stage. Come off stage and do what you want, inject crack into your eyeballs if you want, just don't do it while were working.

Again after a gig one night, an argument started because Lee was speeding his face off. I think me and Joss agreed that when Lee was on amphetamine it effected his playing. I think Joss was living at mine at the time too. So like I said, when having words after the gig, Lee's ego came out. Again, because he was off his tits. I seem to remember the argument went on for several hours and at the end of it Lee announced he would be leaving the group, it was totally out of spite, knowing full well we had gigs coming up. Lee just wanted to make a point and he was happy to put the band at ransom to make his point.

Two days later, Webo rang me. We'd all agreed at this point we'd had enough of Lee, however Lee had come down from taking speed and decided he wasn't leaving the band. I however, had other ideas and if the truth be told, Joss agreed with me. I remember saying to Webo no uncertain terms that Lee had left voluntarily and he wasn't coming back. This put Webo in a predicament as him and Lee were good mates. Fortunately for us however, Ian at this point had put an advert on Facebook, which got a massive response, also in the meantime, Grey, Webo's brother, agreed to fill in till the new guitarist was ready. Sounds good on paper.

The auditions for the new guitarist was at Top House in Hessle. Jason and Sheila ran it at the time and just agreed to let us use the back room for the audition. In return we would throw them a gig later down the line. Again, as with Ian's audition, several guitarists were given an allocated time and the list of four songs to learn of different genres. Again, the theory behind it was if they cannot learn four songs in a week, how are they going to be able to gig. The day of the audition came and as expected, two guitarists dropped out. That left about five. One obviously wasn't good enough and there were a few others who were okay, but not quite right.

One guy rang me to say he was on his way and that he'd be there in half an hour, he turned up two hours late, hadn't learnt any of the songs and still expected himself to be good enough to join The Fixers, the thing was I knew him, although he did not realize it was Joe from Dirty Deeds.

There was one guitarist though that shone and even from the first song, it was obvious that this guy had something. Not only did he look the part but his playing was amazing, if the truth be told, far superior to Lee's. The only thing is I cannot remember his name to this day, however he was half Dutch. It was obvious to all The Fixers that he was getting the job, however, out of fairness we let the other guitarists have their auditions.

In the meantime, Grey was filling in and we managed to salvage all our gigs. Even though Grey didn't necessarily know the set, we managed to cater around him. In some cases, however, we did not have a full set list. This came to head one night at the Red Lion in Driffield, not only was we late going on, about half past nine, we finished about half past eleven. The landlady was away and there were two young girls on the bar. One of them promptly told me we can't pay you in full, because you finished early. I agreed with this kid if we continued to midnight, we would get the full price, but as a result, not only did we have to repeat some of the same set, we also spent half an hour taking the piss out the bar staff.

As you can imagine, the two teenage dolly birds were not best pleased. The next day we got a phone call from the Land lady and these two girls had milked it for everything with her, as a result we were banned from The Red Lion. On a lighter note, The Red Lion is now a derelict pub as it soon went under and is boarded up in Driffield.

Grey's intervention really got The Fixers out of a hole. I must admit, it was good fun playing with Grey again. Grey also seemed to be happy doing the odd gig, that was until he decided he wanted to be the fulltime guitarist for The Fixers.

From the start I thought this would be a bad idea. Grey was a great guitarist and a great guy, but I knew from The New Retros, Grey had his tantrums if he could not get his own way.

Also, we'd auditioned the Dutch guy, as a result of telling Grey we've got someone already, Grey rang me up on a Saturday at two o'clock in the afternoon, to tell me he wasn't doing that nights gig and added he wouldn't fill in anymore because he felt jaded basically. I'd rung around everyone I knew to try and get a guitarist for that night, but nothing. I tried to cancel the gig and get a replacement group, at this point Webo, Joss and Ian are addiment they're doing it. I felt however, it was a bad idea without a lead guitarist. I told Webo to cancel the gig and then I made my way to North Wales, where I was due to go on holiday with my other half.

In the end Webo, Joss and Ian did the gig, but by all accounts it was a poor show, they did not get paid properly and obviously we never got rebooked.

Chapter Seventeen- The Fixers Part Four

I'd decided to audition the group for a few agents. The auditions were out of town and of course Webo didn't want to do it. I think Webo saw it as gigging for nothing, I had a different view however. A lot of these agents had contacts at the caravan parks, which meant work five nights a week, also we could get on the wedding circuit as well at the corporate circuit, where the cheques were a lot bigger.

Again it was agreed, they would do the auditions, however the audition was somewhere in West Yorkshire, in the middle of nowhere. I remember hiring a van whilst Joss drove. The trouble was Webo had put the dampener on the gig before we had even left Hull. Bearing in mind Ian was new to the game, he believed Webo that it was a waste of time, that nothing would come of it and as a result decided to get pissed in the car on the way to the audition. To add insult to injury, Ian also swore down the microphone as well as getting a bucket from the back stage area and proceeded to put it on his head whilst he was singing.

For some reason, we didn't get the audition. I wasn't happy at all. More so with Webo than Ian, as he had put the dampener on it. I always believe there is no such thing as "it's just another gig." Every gig is special as it has to be. You don't know who's going to see you and want you for their wedding, I always feel you must give 100% at every performance, or don't bother. Like I said, nothing came of the audition other than the manager saying "I don't know why your singer got so pissed and we'll ring you if we need you." Needless to say, we never got the call.

Ian's behavior was getting more obnoxious at gigs. I'd made it clear when he'd joined The Fixers, no drinking at rehearsals or gigs, but that rule seemed to go straight out the window when he had got settled into the group. On top of this, like I'd said earlier, some of the people he was bringing to the shows, were gobshites. On one occasion, we was playing on Beverly Road, when one of his mates tried to glass someone. Again, we were never asked back.

The one gig that sticks out as the biggest show up, was at The Norland in Hessle. To be fair, Ian had rang me about two weeks before the gig to see if he could cancel because Hull City were playing Arsenal in the FA cup final. In hindsight, I should have just agreed and cancelled the gig, but again I always felt cancelling bookings was bad for business. Ian then asked "Is it okay if I have a drink then, so I can watch the match?" which I agreed but told him not to get too blathered for the gig. Big mistake.

I seem to remember there was some sort of festival going on at The Norland that day. It might have been Norfest or it could have been Hessle feast. Anyways, we get to the venue and get set up, only Ian is a no show. Eventually Joss gets hold of him and he's at home watching the football with his moron mates. Joss agrees to go pick him up for the gig. By the time Joss gets back to the Norland it's obvious Ian is worse for wear. God only knows what he had had, but from what Joss was telling me, when a decision went against Hull, Ian threw a can at the telly and smashed it.

We crack on with the gig and Ian can hardly stand, let alone sing, but we managed to get through the first set. Fiona, the Land lady of The Norland at the time, collared me at the break. "Your singers a bit pissed Robbo." And of course I had to play it down explaining that he was a big Hull City fan and it was the FA final and that I would keep an eye on him.

Things went worse from there. During the second set, Ian's slurring and swearing down the microphone, also as it was a festival, two coppers came into the pub. At this point Ian shouts down the microphone something along the lines of "We're Hull City and we take coke, fuck the coppers." Even the bar staff came up to us and said that that had to be cut out straight away. It was a right showing up. I turned to Webo and said "Weeb, you do the singing and stick Ian in a taxi." At which point Webo defiantly said " I'm not singing." There was nothing I could do. So in the middle of the second set, I cancelled the gig. I went up to Fiona and apologized, then told her not to pay us. At this point, Ian's kicking off like fuck. In the end, I think Joss took him home.

The next day, Norland cancelled all gigs we had with them. Within half an hour of getting the call, I had another call from Four in Hand on Holderness Road and again they were cancelling.

In the space of twenty four hours, we'd lost over a thousand pounds worth of gigs. Two days later, there was a band meeting at Webo's. Ian sat there like butter wouldn't melt, he then said he was sorry from the trouble he had caused, however I knew full well he wasn't sorry at all. He just didn't want to be kicked out of The Fixers. The look in his eyes told me there was no remorse. I think the next gig was at Walton Street Club, again Ian had a drink but he didn't kick the arse out of it. Before we went on I collared him and tried to explain to him that that can't happen again ever. He shrugged his shoulders, agreed with me and then walked off like he didn't give a fuck.

Another occasion where Ian was not at his best, was my wedding. The ceremony was fine and he turned up with his then girlfriend Tyler, however once we got back to the reception they both downed a bottle of red and white wine that was on all the tables.

Later, I was also told they had been on Mcat. There was family politics going on when I got married to Julie, therefore I decided it best all round that I would hire door staff for the reception. I was glad I did. It wasn't long before Tyler was throwing up in the toilets, as a result, the door staff kicked her out. Soon, Ian's protesting about Tyler to the door staff, as a result, he got thrown out. From there he's trying to ring me on my wedding day to get back in the venue. He's even asking Joss to get hold of me, bearing in mind, I've got 130 guests. I'm outside at this point talking to my new father-in- law, whom I didn't necessarily get on with. Ian is in the background shouting his mouth off all the time, well within earshot. "Fucking this fucking that." All because I can't and won't get him back in the venue.

On top of that, he decides to tell everyone he is leaving the band. All I can say, my wedding day was a complete success, down to the weather, but also, I was right to get door staff because I have no doubt Ian would have ended up starting something.

Unsurprisingly, the Dutch guitarist we had at the time, decided to leave. To be fair, he said he was relocating to Bristol, however again, we had to go through the rigmarole of finding a new guitarist. Initially, I had the number of a young kid called Anthony. I'd met his Mother in the Post office of all places and she explained she did photography for bands. After a few chats on the phone, I agreed to a photoshoot, only to have to cancel because we were going to be a man down.

At that point, she suggested her Son, Anthony. We did auditions at the Schooner Pub in Boothferry. I agreed to pick Anthony up, all he had to do was learn the set list, about thirty songs. Before the audition, Anthony rang me and told me he'd only learnt half the songs. Then on the day of the audition when I picked him up, he told he'd only learnt about ten songs. When it got to the audition, he told the band he'd only learnt three songs, it turns out he hadn't learnt fuck all. The whole thing was a waste of time, however, it'll become apparent later on why I'm mentioning Anthony. Anthony was to become a key member of The Jackdaws. In the meantime, the door was open for Lee to return.

Ian had managed to get a gig at The Guildhall in Hull. It was a wedding, however because it was in a Government building, all the gear had to be PAT tested. Basically what this means, it was to be certified fit for use by an electrician. This includes guitars, leads, microphones, amplifiers and a PA.

The good news was the best man's brother was a sparky. It was agreed he would PAC test all the equipment for free as a favor. Knowing what I knew about The Fixers, I could not trust them to sort it out themselves. I made an arrangement for all the PAT testing of all the equipment to be done at my house at the same time. On the night of the test, the sparky turned up only it wasn't the best man's Brother, it was his mate from work. Long story, short, all the equipment was certified and perfectly fine to use.

The gig at the Guildhall came and went well. This was even though, there was still some underlying resentments from the Norland gig. After this, I thought no more about it, that was until, I got a debt recovery letter through the post.

The sparky that came, I assumed wrongly was PAT testing the gear as a favor. Wrong. I got on the phone to Ian straight away. Ian being Ian, his response was "I'll sort it, I'll sort it." Two months after this, I got another debt recovery letter, only this time it was in red and they wanted more money. Now bearing in mind I'm a drummer, nothing I play with is electrical, other than the microphone. It was however, all done at my house, which meant in turn I was liable for the whole bill. Again, I got on to Ian and again Ian's response was " I'll sort it, I'll sort it."

A third letter came and at this point I had had enough. Not of the bill, but I had had enough of The Fixers. I had had enough of the arguments, also I was struggling to get bookings because of the reputation the band had. None of us were getting on and it didn't matter what I did, there was always someone in the band to tell me I was doing something wrong. A close friend of mine called Mike Rodgers, a musician in his own right, once told me "Running a band is like having four Girlfriends. No one is ever happy." Mike wasn't wrong. Every one of The Fixers, I felt were like spoilt petulant children. No one ever said "Well done". More than this, no one ever did anything for the group except me. If I wasn't there to do it, then it would not get done, however every one of them were quick to pick up if I made a mistake. The truth be told, I had had enough for some time before I left. But like any toxic relationship, you keep holding out in the hope that things will improve, which they never did. In all honesty, I should've left about a year before I did.

The night of the last gig I did with The Fixers, was at the Crow's Nest in Longhill. I told the group I was leaving, I also told the group, out of the gig money I was going to pay the bailiffs bill. Again, Ian protested "I'm going to sort it, I'm going to sort it." At which point I told him enough was enough and it was beyond that now. Ian at this point was with a girl and she had bought her parents along to the gig. I remember telling them that I was leaving and the Dad saying that Ian could hardly remember half the gigs he had done because he was off his head. I agreed and said "Well this is the thing isn't it."

The gig finished and I made a levy for the bar to get the money, I then packed down as quickly as I could, collared Joss at the door and give him the band money minus my cut and the money for the debt. I think there was about sixty quid left over. Driving home down Holderness Road and I get a text from Ian. "You best be leaving the band cunt. You money grabbing jack bastard." I pulled over and was this close to driving back to The Crow's Nest to fill in Ian. I sat there livid for five minutes and came to the conclusion he wasn't worth it. Rightly or wrongly. Instead of turning round, I decided I was that sick of The Fixers I would cancel all the gigs I booked. This was every gig that was booked anyway.

I remember telling Webo I was leaving the group and our friendship at that point had been under so much strain, he was nonchalant about my exit. This was the real travesty of The Fixers. The biggest strength of the group was the relationship onstage and off, between me and Webo. This was also the thing that split and drove the group apart. Both Webo and me, vying for the top job. After I left The Fixers, it was like an ugly divorce. Not one of them would speak to me again for at least five years. The thing that really burns me though, was Joss. We'd been at school together and both of us had been through so much, including Joss living with me and Julie, when he broke up with his then girlfriend Kayleigh.

Initially, Joss tried to keep in touch, however he got a new girlfriend whom I quite liked, only on a brotherly level. Joss read the signals wrong and assumed wrongly that I would try it on. I don't know why he thought I would do this to him, other than poison him from other areas of The Fixers. The last night I saw Joss, he came to mine and we got stuck into a bottle of Jack. Again, we started arguing and he left mine in the small hours and drove home.

Over the years, I've tried numerous attempts to make contact, but I also know once Joss had made his mind up about somebody, nobody will change it. This is his loss, not mine, but if he ever came to read this, know there will always be a double Jack Daniels and coke with his name on and a Led Zepplin album to play.

Chapter Eighteen - The Jackdaws

After leaving The Fixers, I was completely jaded. I was addiment I never wanted to play drums again. I remember Grey coming around to cut the grass and telling him how I felt. His words to me were "You're saying that now, but I promise you down the line, you will get the bug to play live again." He went on to say, he knew how I felt because he'd been there. At the time I didn't believe him, but then I forgot it's Grey and he's always right.

As I'd cancelled all The Fixers gigs, they went from gigging every weekend to once every couple of months almost overnight. They'd also changed the name from The Fixers to The Substitutes. In the meantime, I just enjoyed the break. It was empowering not having to deal with other people's stresses. A lot of these stresses were caused by substance abuse and inflated egos.

Around this time, there was a new land lord in my local pub, The Admiral. Mark and Carol had always been great publicans, however they were new to the area. They knew I'd had problems with The Fixers and they knew I'd left them in the shit, but they always fought my corner, whenever The Substitutes came in asking for a gig. Turning them down, left, right and center.

One afternoon, I was having a Guinness with my Dad, when Mark collared me. They were hosting a competition called Pub Factor. One of the judges had let them down, they asked me if I would judge. Pub factor was a singing competition, run by a few breweries. They needed a panel of three to four judges, I was happy to help out, like I said Mark and Carol had always been good to me. Not only this, the Guinness was that good, it was as if it had come from St James' gate.

It was a week night and I turned up to judge the competition in my suit. One of the judges, I vaguely knew, the other was a singer I'd never met and to be fair, never seen since, however she worked for one of the agencies. The night went well, there was some talent there but nothing really was standing out, until this kid got up called Adam.

I remember clearly thinking he looked like a singer. He was a good looking guy, he had long dark hair and he was smartly dressed. Almost like a young Paul Rodgers in a suit. He got up and did one song and it was Bon Jovi's "You give love a bad name." I didn't know it on the night, but I would go on to form the Jackdaws with this guy. Some singers obviously did not get through. Some got through with the skin of their teeth, but I happily put Adam through. At the end of the night all the judges had a drink and as I was leaving I collared Adam. I told him I liked what he did, I also told him he looked like a singer and he looked like he deserved to be there. Also, I said next time I want to see you sing a free number or a classic rock number. And that was that.

That night was a success and I got asked to judge again the

following week. Again, I turned up in my suit determined to look the part. And again, it was the same judges as the week before. The usual got up and sang, only this time when Adam got up the track he picked kept slipping. Now, as a singer, it would be easy to have a tantrum in the middle of the stage, Adam never. He picked up from where the song was and carried on. Again, the track jumped. And again, Adam just picked up from where the track was. I remember sitting with the other judges just thinking " I can work with this guy." I thought he'd done really well and I gave him full points. All the points system was done discreetly and nobody knew till the end who had won. Also the head judge was Mike. This is where the problem lay, not to go into too much detail but there were politics involved that night. Basically, one of the contestants was a relative of someone important to the judges and although I did not put him through, scores were fiddled in order for him to do well. This in turn meant Adam did not get through. I thought this was a travesty. Adam should definitely have got through.

Not only did he look the part, as a singer all eyes are on you when it goes wrong, and when it went wrong that night with the tracking, most singers I knew would have stormed off whereas Adam ploughed on. Okay, he didn't have a great stage presence at the time, possibly you could argue he needed experience, but then I wasn't looking for the new Steven Tyler. I wanted professionalism and effort. Adam had both of these qualities. Given what had gone on that night with the scoring, I didn't even stop for a drink, however, on the way outside Adam was nursing a pint, you could argue feeling a bit dejected. I told him "I wasn't the only one who thought you should get through tonight, however give me your mobile, I'm going to be putting a band together and you can sing if you want." We changed numbers, however it was a few months before anything happened.

Even though I was enjoying the break, and Christmas had come and gone, Grey's words were true. I was missing the bug of playing. I still had Adam's number and I think it was about January when I called him. It wasn't a long drawn out conversation, I just told him if he wanted to sing for a group I was putting together, he could, however he would need to get his own PA. That was the end of the conversation.

Also, I still had Anthony's telephone number, who had auditioned for The Fixers. On the night of his audition for The Fixers, I remember Anthony, again feeling dejected because he hadn't got the job, but also he said that a lot of the songs we did were easy to play on bass. He went onto suggest we sack Joss an put him on bass. Of course, once Joss heard about this he was livid. Anyway, I contacted Anthony and told him I was putting a group together and it was going to be a professional group. I asked him if he wanted to come in on bass and he jumped at the chance.

I can't remember how it all came about, but it wasn't long before the new group had a few songs and we'd all met each other. Our only Achillies' heel was we did not have a lead guitarist. This is where Anthony came into his own. He met a kid called Chris at Humber Street Sesh a couple of weeks before he joined us, he gave me his number and I called him.

Chris and Anthony were both the same age, both late teens, early twenties, however both had been bought up in different worlds. The things they both had in common, both were music fans, both were keen to play and both just wanted to gig. We arranged an audition for Chris at my house and I gave him four songs to learn. Again, the theory behind this was if Chris can't learn four songs in a week, how's he going to learn a full set.

I was in on my own when I let Chris in for his audition at my house. It was strange but refreshing to see him, he had a Jimmy Page look about him, yet he was only twenty, maybe twenty one. Most twenty one year old kids I knew, knew nothing about music, were trying to be gangsters and generally were morons. I went onto explain to Chris that we'd be earning good money, however the money would be crap at first. Also I explained to him there was a strict no drink, no drugs policy. I.e. no drugs at gigs or practice and if he didn't follow this, he would be sacked. I did say, however, after the gig I'm happy for you to inject crack into your eyeballs if it suits you. Just not while were working. Chris didn't seem phased about this at all. It was obvious he wasn't a drug user, in fact I think he felt pleased to be auditioning for something more professional. I think generally, the school bands he'd been in didn't necessarily know what they was doing or take it seriously.

The rest of the guys turned up and we went through the four songs together in my living room. Not only had Chris learnt all the songs to perfection, his solos were great. In the interests of fairness, Anthony, Adam and myself stepped outside for a minute to discuss. It was obvious to all of us, he was our guitarist. Chris struck me that while his mates were out chasing girls and playing football and taking drugs, he would have been sat in his bedroom learning the originals Blue's tunes from the masters. I don't just mean Eric Clapton and Jimmy Page, but also the true originals, such as Howling Wolf and Robert Johnson.

The next job was to pick the set list. Every one of them in the group were a novices. None had gigged and all were happy to be there. To be honest, this in itself was refreshing, because it meant it wasn't all about the money. I addressed the group and told them they would all need suits as we would be playing a lot of working men's clubs and I wanted us all to look uniformed. I reiterated the fact there was a no drug, no drink policy, all agreed they didn't have a problem.

The next job was to pick the set list. The way I saw it, everyone would have a say but I would have the final say. The songs we picked needed to be well known songs from the sixties and seventies. It was no good picking some obscure Pink Floyd B-side. The songs we played needed to get people up and dancing. If they're dancing, they're drinking more, if they're drinking more, the venue is happy and if the venue is happy, we get rebooked. It was that simple. Again, because they were all new to the circuit, I had to instill into them, if we make a mistake live, don't worry about it, half the time Joe public can't hear it, then just find out where you are in the song and pick it up from there. Unless the Joe public were purists, they wouldn't hear a bung note in a Beatles tune or Stone's number.

Because they were all new to the circuit, I had to build them up. I didn't want the pressure of a booked, paid gig, if they'd never done it before. The answer to this was an open mic night. Firstly, we would learn four song acoustically at my house, after this we would play it live in a studio, once we had mastered the song in the studio, the best three numbers we would take to an open mic night at Ferriby and play live. It was a great introduction for the band, playing live together. Like I said, there was no pressure and it got all of the group used to playing live as a team. We went on like this for a few months until I felt we were good enough.

As a band, we were staring to gel. Adam had bought his own PA from his sister (Torie whom was a singer in her own right). Also, he had bought a monitor. Chris had all his own gear, the problem was with Anthony. Even at the first practice, it was down to Chris to get Anthony a bass amp. I remember pulling Anthony up on this. I told him it wasn't down to Chris to sort his bass amp. All the time, he was looking at me like I was one of his wanker teachers from school. I soon picked up on this and I had to reassure him I wasn't one of the wanker teachers from school by telling him to wipe this stupid grin off his face before I knocked his face through the wall. This had the desired effect and got his attention. As frustrating as it was, Anthony needed to be told several times before he would do anything for himself. By the same token, Anthony didn't have it on a silver platter. The fact was, Anthony's equipment was shit. He didn't have the money or the means to get anything else. It just so happens at this time, I was working as a minder at an escort agency in Hull. This meant I had access to some funds. (Dirty Laundry- Confessions of an Escort Agency Minder, available on Amazon.) I agreed, I would lay out for a new bass amp and bass guitar. Anthony agreed that it would come out of his gig money. I drove him to Doncaster to

Electro music and got him kitted out.

The first gig we did was a Thursday night in the Admiral. I agreed with Mark and Carol, we would do the gig for 60 quid, plus a pint of Guinness each. As first gigs go, again there wasn't much pressure because of the fact most of the people we were playing for, were our mates. The other thing, it was a week night, it was however the night before we played our first proper paid gig at Ferriby social club. So playing the Admiral was a good warm up.

The gig at Ferriby also went well. Because we had done the open mic night several times, it meant that the venue and the songs were not to taxing on the band. I should also mention, the name of the group, Adam came up with the name for the group, it was the Jackdaws. After the show, we all piled back to mine. I had to sort the money out with the band plus I wanted us all to have down time together. Again, we didn't get paid much for our first proper gig, I think it was about a hundred and thirty pounds. I remember clearly paying Chris in front of his mum and apologizing that the money was crap, however I promised it would get better.

The look in Chris' eyes, it was like he could not believe he had been paid at all for playing music at a venue. Again, this was a world away from The Fixers. Had I handed over just over thirty quid each to any of them, every one of them would have been moaning. The Jackdaws was the world away from The Fixers. Everyone was just happy to play and grateful of it. There was a certain naivety to The Jackdaws, which I knew I had to nurture properly in order to get full potential out of the group.

Because I had all the contacts, it didn't take long before the diary was getting full. Gigs were coming in thick and fast, plus the money was starting to improve. We still had teething problems with Anthony, but he was nothing that couldn't be resolved through a stern talk or a late night chat after a gig over a beer. It was the usual stuff, get to gigs on time, look the part, also Anthony was a pothead at the time. I had to do the big Brother talk around drugs, just so he was educated as to what he was putting in his body.

I also started to notice there was a few tensions creeping in because of this between him and Adam. Again, I quickly nipped it in the bud, I didn't want it escalating into something that The Fixers became. The biggest problem we had with Anthony I felt, was his attitude to money. He was so tight, he didn't breath out. Even early on at practices, he would be arguing over a few pence change, after we had all chipped in for the practice room. When he realized I was not going to give him any leeway regarding the funds I had laid out for him for his new bass and amp, he wasn't happy. It meant he did about six or seven gigs where he didn't get paid. I knew full well however, if I'd of given Anthony an inch, he would have took a yard.

All the problems in the Jackdaws were nothing compared to what I had been through. Again, after every gigs the band would pile back to mine to put the world to rights over a beer and a joint. Adam and Anthony would be best mates by then. It was like nothing had happened at the gig and were getting on like a house on fire, until the next gig. Adam also, was very generous with his mates, all would pile back to mine after a gig, the only difference being, all the mates Adam knew were not dickheads. To this day, I am still mates with some of Adam's mates because of some of those late night parties.

One party in particular, was in the middle of summer and we were playing the Admiral in Hessle. I said to Adam I didn't want a houseful after the gig, but the usual were welcome. The only trouble was it didn't feedback to Anthony.

That night, half the pub, which felt like half of Hessle, came back to mine. In hindsight, there might of not been that many people there, there might have been thirty or so, however it went on until about eleven o'clock the next morning. My neighbors at the time, Tom and Leslie, were very good about it, even though I had kept them up all night. (With the nights gig money I got Tom and Leslie a voucher for a meal at a Greek restaurant as a way of apology, which they were more than happy with.) By all accounts the parties were great, we had some great nights, some long discussions and I'll be honest, I made some great friends, mainly through Adam.

As with the other groups, the gigs were starting to come in. I was fortunate in the sense, I still had the contacts from The Fixers, therefore a lot of venues were willing and able to give The Jackdaws a chance. Around this time, I got an email from Hull Daily Mail. It was Vicky Norman asking me if I wanted to do Talent Trail again.

After the fiasco of the last one I did with The Fixers, I sent a long winded response calling fuck out the whole competition. I also mentioned the fact that groups never win it and it is always solo acts. Within a couple of days, I had a phone call from Vicky. Apparently, I was not the only one who had highlighted these discrepancies. As a result, the competition now had a segment for groups as well as a segment for singers. Vicky asked me if I would be interested. After I hung up, I thought about it and I came to the conclusion it would be good exposure. I remember putting it to the band, who had never heard of the competition. Again, this was a bonus, as they did not know to piss and moan about it. The only one who had a beef, was Anthony's mother. I remember her telling me what a waste of time it was when we wasn't being paid. I soon put her in her place and reminded her that it was Anthony's Grandmother that had bought him up and not her.

The first heat was at The Griffin, on Anlaby Road. There were supposed to be five bands playing for two places. In the end, there was only four. I was quietly confident we would get through this round. At this point, we had been playing for well over a year. Also, we were professional in how we carried on, right down to helping each other carry the equipment, getting to the gigs on time, acting appropriately in the venue and most importantly wearing our suits. Having said that, the competition was stiff.

The first group to get up was a hardcore thrash band. After that, a couple of singers, then another group whom we thought would win, then it was us. I remember we did about five or six songs and it was almost as if we had to finish just as we was getting warmed up. We ended the night with our version of The Who's, "My generation". To say I was getting nervous when we came off stage, was an understatement. Not so much for me, I'd been there and done it but for the boys. Every one of them over the last year had worked so hard for me. Every one of them also had done exactly what I'd asked of them. It wasn't for me but I felt they needed some recognition for all their efforts.

At the end of the night, the judges got up to announce who had made it. First of all, the thrash metal kids had got through. Also, a few of the singers. Then, the final act to get through to the next round, The Jackdaws. I remember fist pumping the air. We'd done it. It meant we would be playing the final at Hull City Hall. I also remember thinking, every one of the Jackdaws deserves this. That night, after we got finished, we all piled back to Harry's for a drink and to discuss what two songs we would do in the final. It was like we had it all in front of us. Even though it was a week night, we stayed up till the early hours putting the world to rights.

The anticipation in the lead up to playing the Hull City Hall gig was immense, however, I knew we was good enough. It would be the biggest gig I ever played, it would also be the biggest gig The Jackdaws would ever play. There was a certain amount of pressure to make sure we got it right.

Come the day of the gig and it was a week night. Anthony was the first to arrive at mine, with the rest following suit. We had to get to Hull City Hall that afternoon for the sound check, however, Chris was addiment he wanted to use his own amplifier. I had a word with the staff and they accommodated this.

Soon after the sound check was finished, we headed home for something to eat at to get changed. Not only were the band going, but also a lot of our friends and family. We had to do this for them because they had supported us from day one. Arriving at Hull City

Hall for around half past five, we made our way to the back stage area. Those not in the know, would not realize, the back stage area of Hull City Hall is absolutely massive. More than this, there is also loads of sub rooms all the way up to the roof. I remember sitting back stage in the band area and thinking to myself ' This must be the room that Kieth Moon, the drummer from The Who, did a line of coke off a groupies breast, before he went on to play wearing a dress.' It was literally the stuff of dreams.

The show started and I must admit, I was restless and keen to get on with it. The first group got up and it was the thrash rockers, then there was two singers, after that another group and again two more singers. Then it was our turn. I collared all the lads and I remember telling them clearly "Opportunities like this don't come often. Enjoy it and dare to dream." I think most of them took it on board. We got introduced and entered the stage wearing our suits. Normally, a big event didn't bother me, but that was working men's clubs and pubs. Looking out onto the audience and the place was full. The best thing I could do, was to just get on with it.

Our first number was " Twist and shout" by The Beatles. The number went down really well and we was really tight, probably because of our nerves. I even remember during the song, dropping one of my drum sticks, however it wasn't a problem as I had a stick bag next to me at the time as I normally do, plus nobody noticed.

After we finished the first song, we all decided we would take our jackets off at the same time in unison. This received a wolf whistle from the crowd. Both Adam and myself acknowledged the whistle and said "Thank you" down the mic. Then, Adam turned to me and said " It was for me." I really wanted to say something next, however I knew it would make Adam look a cunt if I said it. What I wanted to say way " Nah mate, it was for me, my Mam's in." this would have got a great reaction. Either way, I bottled it.

Never the less, we soon got stuck in our second number, "Jumping Jack Flash." By the stones. Again, we rocked it up a bit, including an extended guitar solo towards the end. Every one of us was on fire. I could not have asked for a better performance.

Before too long, our set was over. It seemed the irony of it was as soon as you get warmed up, it was time to get off. We got a good applause as we left the stage. Now all we had to do was wait for the result. All of us were shattered and thirsty when we came off stage. I felt it was my responsibility to get everyone a drink. I nipped to the performance area and got four bottles of water, handed them out and opened mine last. For the next hour or so, I spent half the time back stage, the other half, with our friends and family. Soon it was time to find out who had won.

We were all lined up in our groups and called to the stage. I remember saying to The Jackdaws " Look lads, we should have this in the bag, however if for some reason we've not won, remember to act graciously, clap your hands and pat the other groups on the back." The results were announced and we had not won.

A group calling themselves Knocking Shop. Had been given the honor. They were the last group on and were doing loads of cocaine back stage before they got up. Also, they had bought a large crowd with them. Did I feel cheated? In a way I suppose I did, but not as much as the people who had come to support us thought we had been cheated.

Turns out, the judging was down to one guy, even though there was a panel of judges. This individual was something to do with Humber Street Sesh. From what I can gather, he used his position to leverage the other judges, because he wanted Knocking Shop for his festival. Also, from what I can gather, when he had done this, another judge, who was from Goth and Davy, was not happy and walked out before the result was read. We later learnt, there was one point between us and the winners. Again, you could argue it was fiddled.

Despite the rights and wrongs, the rest of the night the Jackdaws went back to Harry's bar along with our friends and family. Even my neighbors Tom and Leslie had come to watch us.

Okay, we had not won, but we had played Hull City Hall. It was a great coup and it would set us in great stead for gigs to come. Coincidently, one of the judges ran Kingston artists and was forever giving us work. As for Knocking shop, apparently they'd formed three days before the competition. Not long after the competition, they played Humber street sesh, then disappeared into the insignificance. We never did find out what happened to them.

The rest of the night was a complete piss up, eventually ending at mine, where only my neighbors Tom and Leslie, Adam and myself were still standing. In hindsight, I think I did okay.

The Jackdaws today are a different beast. There's only one original member, Adam. And there had been several lineup changes. I was the first to leave, however, to this day we are all still mates after a fashion. Adam and me meet up regularly, the other two are a phone call away.

Some of the best night I had, were playing in groups. Whether it was the gig itself or the after show party. Also, some of the closest mate I have are Musos. The ones that get to read this, if I have mentioned you, please hold no grudge as I like to think it's a honest account. I feel I have written from the heart. As for my next project, I hear Oasis are reforming, I'm sure they could use a drummer.

If you have enjoyed reading this book, please feel free to leave a review, unless it was crap, in that case, don't put anything. Lastly, please check out my other work on Amazon or at my website " Michaelsrobinsonauthor.com"

Goodnight and God bless.

Printed in Great Britain
by Amazon